*"Fair thoughts and
happy hours attend on you!"*

*William Shakespeare*

We hope you have seen many memorable sights on
our *London Times* journey. May this gift always
remind you of the time we've spent together.

***Tally-ho!***

*London Times*

# ·LONDON·

## A CITY REVEALED

AA Publishing

Text adapted from *Explorer London* by Christopher Catling, first published by AA Publishing, 1994

Produced by AA Publishing

Published by AA Publishing (a trading name of Automobile Association Developments Limited, whose registered office is Millstream, Maidenhead Road, Windsor, Berkshire SL4 5GD; registered number 1878835)

Visit the AA Publishing Web site at www.theAA.com

ISBN 0 7495 1584 8
A CIP catalogue record for this book is available from the British Library.

Copy editor Penny Phenix

Colour separation by Fotographics Ltd

Printed and bound in China

p1 *Old London as depicted by the Dutch artist deWit;*
p2/3 *The Great Fire of London, 1666, from the Dutch School*

# ·CONTENTS·

# ·INTRODUCTION·

ondon is a huge city, steeped in history and yet vibrant and uniquely entertaining. The heart of the city is also the powerhouse of the nation – the magnificent Houses of Parliament, dominating a wide reach of the River Thames; Buckingham Palace, the London home of the sovereign, standing at the end of The Mall, its tree-lined processional thoroughfare; the 'square mile' known as the City, where the stately Bank of England presides over the financial giants of commerce and industry. Here too is the religious heart of the capital, with the strikingly beautiful St Paul's Cathedral and ancient Westminster Abbey.

In every part of the city history rubs shoulders with the cut and thrust of modern life, and much of London's fascination comes from its enormous contrasts – one day looking to future concerns of international importance, amidst the constant hum of city traffic, the next harking back to the past with centuries-old royal pageantry, complete with horse-drawn carriages and colourful costumes.

Beyond the city centre there is still more to discover, in the villages that have retained their own special character despite being swallowed up in the urban sprawl. There are royal palaces and fine classical mansions, once surrounded by open countryside; there are leafy streets of Georgian houses where blue plaques mark the former residences of great luminaries; there are wonderful art galleries and splendid museums.

But grand buildings and splendid events alone do not make a city, and much of London's charm comes from its cosmopolitan character – in cultural enclaves such as Soho's Chinatown, in events such as the Caribbean carnival in Notting Hill, from the talent and inventiveness of the street entertainers and from the general mélange on its busy streets. This is just a small sample of the delights that London has to offer – there is much, much more.

*Despite burning down London in*
*AD 60, queen Boudicca of the Iceni*
*tribe is commemorated by a stirring*
*bronze statue on Victoria Embankment*

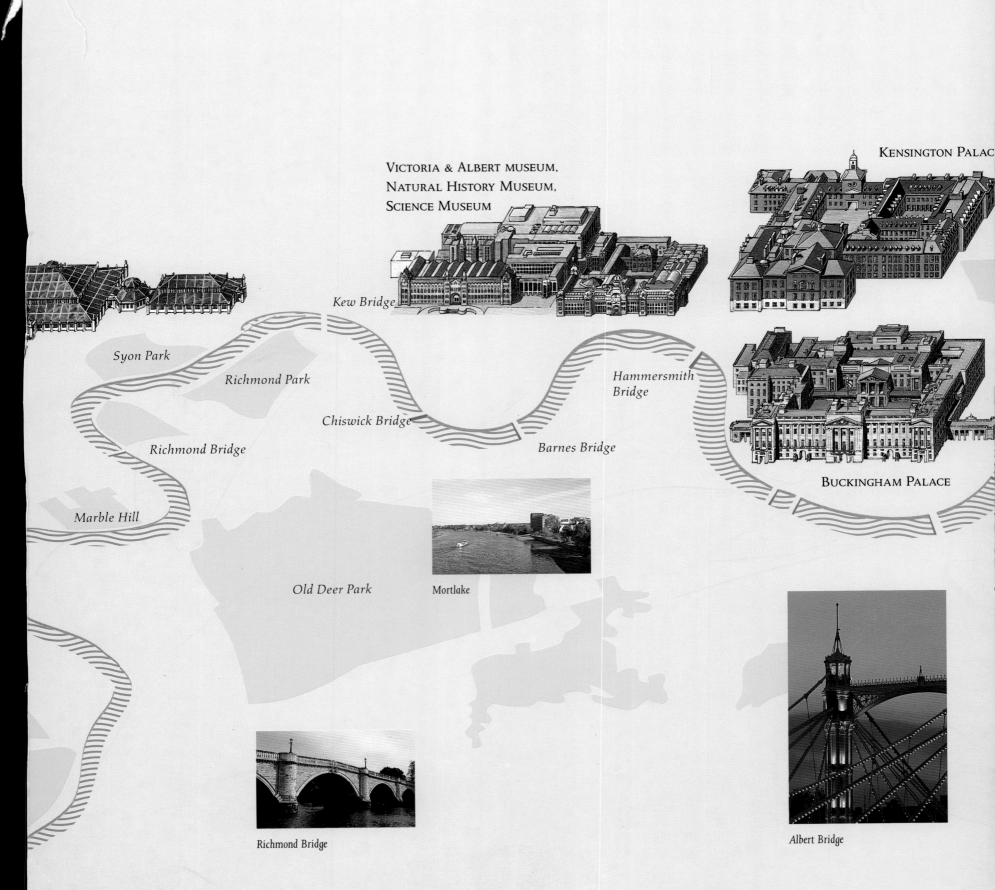

VICTORIA & ALBERT MUSEUM,
NATURAL HISTORY MUSEUM,
SCIENCE MUSEUM

KENSINGTON PALAC

*Kew Bridge*

*Syon Park*

*Richmond Park*

*Hammersmith
Bridge*

*Chiswick Bridge*

*Barnes Bridge*

*Richmond Bridge*

BUCKINGHAM PALACE

*Marble Hill*

*Old Deer Park*

*Mortlake*

Richmond Bridge

Albert Bridge

# The Thames

TO TRAVEL ON THE THAMES IS TO MAKE A VOYAGE through a nation's history. From the magnificent Tudor palace at Hampton Court, the river winds in great loops into the heart of the capital. It flows beneath the walls of the Houses of Parliament and reflects the forbidding outline of the Tower of London in its waters. From the Pool of London it descends through a regenerated Docklands and Canary Wharf, passes Greenwich – site of another royal palace – and flows beyond the Flood Barrier at Woolwich, that powerful symbol of security, before escaping to the sea.

London owes its very existence to Father Thames and, only now, after too many years of complacency and neglect, is the river once again beginning to regain some of its former grandeur and respect as the vital artery of the city. Fish and other wildlife have returned to its increasingly clean waters, innovative ideas are being aired for new, living bridges, river cruises are thriving and the long-awaited Thames Path, running the whole length of the river, is now open.

8

### THE ROYAL BOTANIC GARDENS

Boats at Hampton Court

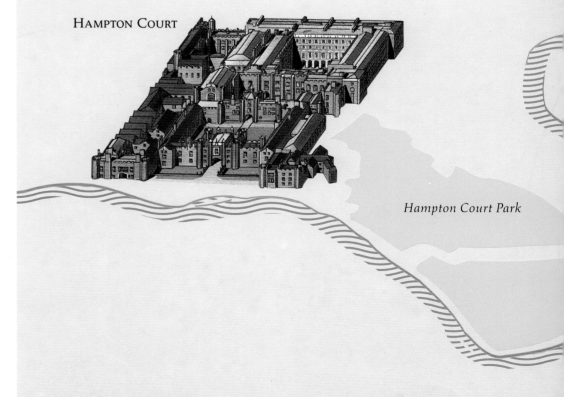

### HAMPTON COURT

*Hampton Court Park*

Once London's greatest thoroughfare, the River Thames meanders its way through the city, spanned by tens of splendid and varied bridges

*Victoria Park*

Thames River Bus

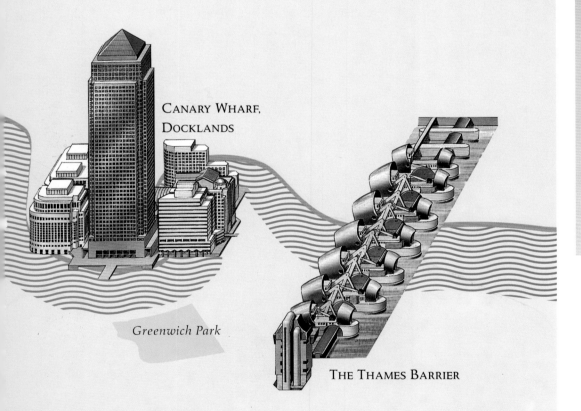

CANARY WHARF,
DOCKLANDS

*Greenwich Park*

THE THAMES BARRIER

Greenwich Old Observatory

## THE THAMES PATH

◆

The country's newest and long-awaited National Trail stretches some 180 miles (290km) from the river's source in the hills of Gloucestershire to the new face of east London at the Isle of Dogs. Passing through a huge diversity of landscapes, visiting historic cities, towns and villages, the path offers the unique opportunity of travelling alongside the river for the whole of its length.

Enjoy the scenic and tranquil countryside of the Cotswolds or the water meadows outside Oxford – contrasting superbly with the bustle of this most historic of towns. The path continues through some of the most prestigious areas of the Home Counties, places like Henley-on-Thames, scene of one of the country's notable annual occasions – the Henley Regatta. Passing through the Royal County of Berkshire, with Windsor the major site, the trail continues into the affluent stockbroker belt of Surrey, meeting up with sections of the River Wey Navigation. Moving eastwards the path offers the ideal vantage point for the annual University Boat Race along the stretch of water near Barnes, where rowers from the University of London regularly practise their skills.

To walk right into the heart of London along the South Bank or the Victoria Embankment is to experience all the sights and sounds of Westminster and beyond, to the imposing grandeur of the Tower of London and the spectacular sight of Tower Bridge. Flowing seamlessly from ancient to modern and back, the path follows the Thames east towards the regenerated Docklands and Canary Wharf before reaching its journey's end, appropriately, opposite the Royal Naval College at Greenwich – a fitting end to so timeless a journey.

*This representation of the River Thames on its way through London is, of course, not to scale; most of the landmarks featured along its route will be found in this book, plus a great many more; to make best use of the three-dimensional illustrations, a degree of artistic licence with regards to positioning has been necessary*

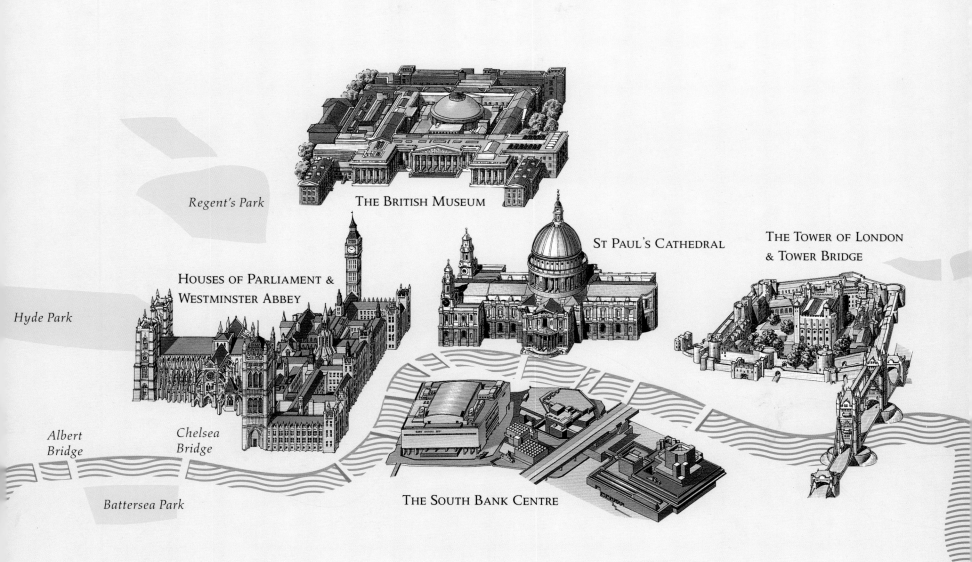

*Regent's Park*

THE BRITISH MUSEUM

ST PAUL'S CATHEDRAL

THE TOWER OF LONDON
& TOWER BRIDGE

HOUSES OF PARLIAMENT &
WESTMINSTER ABBEY

*Hyde Park*

*Albert
Bridge*

*Chelsea
Bridge*

THE SOUTH BANK CENTRE

*Battersea Park*

IMPERIAL WAR MUSEUM

Chelsea Bridge

Cleopatra's Needle, Embankment

Blackfriars Bridge

# ·WEST LONDON·

*W*est London has always been a fashionable place. Many of London's formerly run-down suburbs may have become smart over the last 30 years or so, but Kensington and Knightsbridge addresses were always guaranteed to impress. Historically, the Thames has a lot to do with the popularity of the west because until relatively recently, travelling by water was much easier than any land route, and this wide, gently curving river was London's main thoroughfare. It swept past the royal residences at Windsor Castle and Hampton Court Palace, Richmond and Kew on its way into the city, and where royalty went, the rest of the aristocracy followed. There are a number of splendid mansions along London's western corridor, including Syon House at Isleworth, Ham House at Richmond and Chiswick House.

The river was also a great inspiration to the artistic community, and many of Britain's greatest writers, poets and atists gravitated towards west London's riverside 'villages' — particularly Chiswick. West London is also know for its parks and gardens and for this, too, we can thank former royalty — not that the public had access to it in those days. Hunting was one of the favourite recreations of the monarchs and aristocracy, and most of today's lovely parks were royal hunting preserves, from which ordinary folk were excluded on pain of death. Eventually, more enlightened monarchs threw open these lovely green spaces for everyone to enjoy and they provide a wonderful breathing space away from city traffic. One of the biggest stretches of green in the entire capital is provided by the twin parks of Hyde Park and Kensington Gardens and the adjacent Kensington Palace Gardens. Further out are Syon Park, Bushy Park (adjacent to Hampton Court Palace), Richmond Park and Windsor Great Park — not to mention the vast Royal Botanical Gardens at Kew.

*This magnificent staircase leads into Osterley Park, the 16th-century manor house built for the City merchant Sir Thomas Gresham*

# Windsor

OWERING ABOVE THE TOWN ON A CHALK CLIFF, THE castle and its strategic site was first defended by William I (the Conqueror) in 1070. For the next 900 years the building was continually enlarged, growing from a medieval castle to a vast and complex royal palace, taking on its present appearance during the 1820s.

In late November 1992 fire broke out at the castle and by the time it was brought under control some of the State Apartments, hung with many works of art from the royal collections, were reduced to charred ruins. Restoration work, which will cost over £30 million, is underway, but many parts of the castle remain open to the public.

*Troops from the Brigade of Guards, the Queen's personal bodyguard, bring the colour and atmosphere of London pageantry to the town of Windsor*

England's largest castle, one of the favourite homes of the royal family, also has one of the most impressive settings, high above the River Thames

## ETON

◆

Windsor's twin town, this is the home of Eton College, the public school that has produced no fewer than 20 prime ministers, and during term it is inhabited by the students dressed in their distinctive tailcoats and wing collars. The Tudor-style school buildings include a Museum of Eton Life, with displays on the school's history, and a chapel featuring 15th-century wall paintings and stained-glass windows by the contemporary artists John Piper and Evie Hone.

The most impressive of all the castle buildings is St George's Chapel, a masterpiece of Perpendicular Gothic architecture, begun in 1478 and completed in 1511. Ten monarchs are buried here, but the best monument is that in the north-west chapel to Princess Charlotte, who died in childbirth in 1817. It shows the princess ascending to heaven with an angel carrying her stillborn child.

## DOLL'S HOUSE

◆

The star attraction of the State Apartments is Queen Mary's Doll's House, designed by Sir Edwin Lutyens and given to the nation in 1923. The furnishings are designed at one-twelfth lifesize, the plumbing and lighting really work, and several contemporary authors and artists contributed miniature paintings or handwritten books to the library.

*FAR TOP LEFT Eton College, founded in 1440 by Henry VI as a school for poor boys, is now one of Britain's most exclusive public schools*

The elaborate 15th-century stalls are covered in vignettes (animals, jesters, the Dance of Death and Biblical stories) and surmounted by banners of the 26 Knights of the Garter, whose installation has taken place here since 1348.

### WINDSOR GREAT PARK

Much more than an adjunct to the castle and the town, this is an attraction in its own right, or, more accurately, several separate attractions. For the nature lover there are long walks within the acres of parkland, whose vast and ancient oaks are host to many rare butterflies, such as the purple hairstreak, and birds, including woodpeckers. On the south-eastern fringes of the park is the Savill Garden – woodland, formal rose gardens and perennial borders – named after Eric Savill, a former park ranger. The Valley Gardens, just south near Egham, lie along the northern shores of Virginia Water, and are famous for massed flowering shrubs. On the site of the defunct Windsor Safari Park, the Legoland theme park is proving a popular attraction.

*FAR BOTTOM LEFT St George's Chapel is universally hailed as the most outstanding architectural feature of the Windsor Castle complex*

15

### WINDSOR TOWN

The royal theme spills over into the town of Windsor, whose fine old buildings include the Guildhall on the High Street, completed in 1707 by Sir Christopher Wren. Its Tuscan columns on the ground floor do not touch the ceiling – apparently, the town council insisted on having them, but Wren left the gap to prove that they were structurally superfluous. Further up the High Street is St Albans Street, leading to the Royal Mews and an exhibition of the Queen's horses, carriages and state coaches. Part of Windsor Central Station now houses a waxworks museum run by Madame Tussaud's, recreating the scene in 1897 when a special train arrived here to celebrate Queen Victoria's Diamond Jubilee.

Leading out of the town, and extending as far as the Long Walk which skirts Windsor Great Park, is Park Street. This 3 mile (5km) avenue was laid out by Charles I and planted with elms, but the original trees died and were replaced in 1945 with chestnut and plane trees.

*LEFT Outside the castle walls, the town of Windsor has some charming old Georgian streets and a number of attractions of its own*

# Syon House and Park

*The undeniably plain exterior of Syon House is in complete contrast with the sumptuous style and decoration that unfolds within this great mansion*

**S**YON HOUSE, HISTORIC SEAT OF THE DUKES OF Northumberland, presents a grim and uninviting façade, but the battlemented mid-16th century building contains some of the most magnificently decorated rooms in England. They are the work of Robert Adam, who remodelled the interior from 1761, employing costly marbles, gilded statues and classical plasterwork to create a palace fit for one of the country's most powerful aristocratic families.

One of the most intriguing aspects of the house is that some rooms were exclusively a male preserve and others were the domain of the ladies of the house, a state of affairs reflected in the decoration and furnishings. The immensely long but narrow Long Gallery, for example, was designed, according to Adam, to 'afford variety and amusement for the

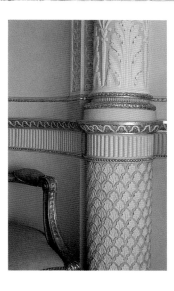

ladies' and is finished in pastel mauve and green with highlights of gold. Around the cornice of the same room, portrait medallions illustrate the lineage of the Dukes of Northumberland, beginning with Charlemagne, the first Holy Roman Emperor, from whom the family claims descent. Several rooms are hung with important family portraits, including works by Gainsborough and Reynolds.

## THE PARK

The extensive grounds of Syon House were landscaped between 1767 and 1773 by Lancelot 'Capability' Brown. A renowned exponent of the 'naturalistic' style, his lakes, lawns and fine specimen trees all serve to create an idyllic version of the natural countryside.

One of the most exciting features of the garden is the Great Conservatory, with a graceful central dome of glass and iron and two curving side wings. This was built between 1820 and 1827 by Charles Fowler (the architect of the original Covent Garden market) and is said to have been a major influence on Joseph Paxton's design for the Crystal Palace. The conservatory contains a variety of different gardens, ranging from the damp fernery to the hot, dry cactus beds.

Also close to the house are formal flower-beds, and a huge garden that is to be devoted entirely to roses. Ultimately it will contain more than 8,000 plants, including many of the older and more unusual varieties. Further away, a walk around the lakes includes many moisture-loving plants, flowering shrubs and unusual trees.

CENTRE *The Ante Room floor is a particularly fine example of Scagliola work, while above, the delicate decoration of the Circular Room is by Robert Adam, c1760*

The Great Hall at Syon House is a
superb example of Robert Adam's
classical style, with exceptional
decorative stucco work by Joseph Rose

## FROM SYON TO THE SCAFFOLD

Several former inhabitants of Syon House ended up in the Tower of London or with their heads on a block. The house was built on the site of a convent, which Henry VIII seized at the Dissolution and gave to the Duke of Somerset. In 1541 Catherine Howard, the king's fifth wife, was imprisoned here, falsely accused of adultery, before her trial and execution. Next was the turn of Somerset himself. He had been appointed Protector to the boy king Edward VI on Henry VIII's death, but was thought to exercise too much power and, accused of conspiracy, he too was beheaded in 1552. Syon then became home to Lady Jane Grey – briefly. Having been proclaimed queen in 1553, she was executed in 1554, the unfortunate victim of the political manoeuvrings of the age.

### OTHER ATTRACTIONS

◆

The Syon estate works hard to keep visitors entertained. Within the grounds, in the former Riding School, is an excellent garden centre with a wide range of plants for house and garden.

The park also includes the London Butterfly House, featuring hundreds of large and colourful species flying freely in a jungle-like setting. There is also a display of giant spiders, scorpions and other creatures designed to induce a frisson of fear.

'Capability' Brown's skill at creating natural-looking landscapes is nowhere more picturesquely demonstrated than at this delightful lake in Syon Park

19

Syon's Great Conservatory is a vast crescent of metal and glass which houses one of the finest private collections of tropical plants in Britain

# Hampton Court

The astronomical clock at Hampton Court was made for Henry VIII in 1540 and adorns the splendid Tudor brickwork of Anne Boleyn's Gateway

𝓗AMPTON COURT, BEGUN BY CARDINAL WOLSEY IN 1515, was originally built as an ecclesiastical palace, not a royal one. The son of an Ipswich butcher, Wolsey rose to fill the highest offices of both Church and State. As the confidant of Henry VIII he took a leading role in the king's complicated marriage affairs. He amassed great wealth and spent it extravagantly, intending Hampton Court to be the most splendid palace in the land. This merely excited the King's envy, and Wolsey decided that it might be wise to present Hampton Court to Henry as a gift, which he did in 1525. The gesture came too late to satisfy the king who, in 1529, had his former friend arrested on a charge of treason and then seized all Wolsey's possessions, including the palace of Whitehall. Disgraced and rejected, the Cardinal soon fell ill, and within a year he was dead.

## COURTYARDS AND KITCHENS

Hampton Court is one of the oldest and most interesting of London's royal palaces. Wren's south wing, badly damaged by fire in 1986, has been superbly restored and the palace, in typical Tudor style, looks like a miniature town which has grown in an organic. unplanned way, unity provided only by the warm reds and browns of the brickwork.

Approach the palace through the Trophy Gate to appreciate its vast scale. No mere royal residence, this also housed a huge retinue of courtiers and followers, as it still does today. The warren of courtyards and buildings to the left contains 'grace and favour' apartments, home to Crown officials, pensioners and dependants of the royal family. The Great Gatehouse, part of the original palace, was altered in the 1770s – originally it was two storeys taller.

RIGHT AND OPPOSITE No description can quite prepare the visitor for the size, the splendour and the historic treasures of Hampton Court Palace

J. Farington R.A del.    Pub. June 1.1793. by J. & J. Boydell.    HAMPTON COURT.    Shakspeare Gallery Pall Mall & Cheapside.    J. C. Stadler sculp.

## THE HAUNTED GALLERY

◆

Ghosts are inevitable in a palace that has seen so much history, but one in particular is said to frequent the so-called Haunted Gallery. It was here that Catherine Howard, the fifth wife of Henry VIII, is said to have broken away from her guards after being arrested for adultery and rushed screaming to appeal to the king who, oblivious to her cries, attended mass in the nearby Chapel Royal. Howard, who continued to protest her innocence, was sentenced to death and beheaded in the Tower in 1542. Since then, a figure in white has been spotted in the gallery on several occasions, uttering an unearthly and piercing scream.

*RIGHT The elegant colonnade of the State Apartments dates from the late 17th century, when the palace was rebuilt for William and Mary*

*BELOW The complexity of the buildings which cluster around the courtyards of the palace can only be properly appreciated from above*

Set into the two side turrets are terracotta roundels depicting Roman emperors, and these and Base Court beyond also date from Wolsey's time. Opposite, Anne Boleyn's gateway is carved with the intertwined initials H and A, for Henry and Anne, celebrating a marriage that lasted only four years before the queen was beheaded.

Clock Court comes next, named after the 16th-century astronomical clock on the gateway's inner side. On the left is Henry VIII's Great Hall, with its splendid oriel window and impressive hammerbeam roof. Beneath the Great Hall are the Tudor Kitchens, with their vast fireplaces and ancient cooking utensils, which hold enormous fascination for visitors and give an insight into the working lives of the servant population of the palace.

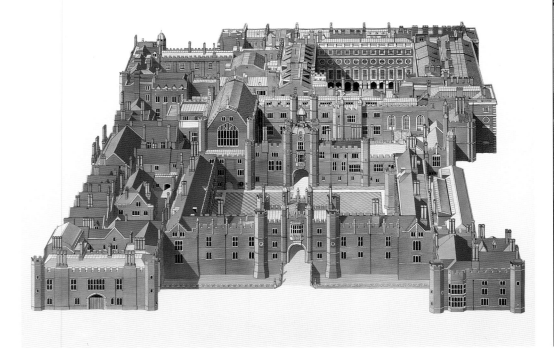

## STATE APARTMENTS

Opposite is Christopher Wren's elegant colonnade, added when the State Apartments were remodelled during the reign of William III (William of Orange, 1689–1702). Wren planned to demolish the whole palace and build a new one, as grand as Versailles, but the royal purse could not stretch to this, and the cosiness of the Tudor buildings remains, providing a strong foil to the rich State Apartments. These are on the first floor, and are decorated with priceless paintings, furnishings, armour and tapestries. Jean Tijou, the French blacksmith, created the ironwork balustrades of the staircases, Grinling Gibbons was responsible for the woodwork and Verrio executed many of the ceiling paintings.

Equally enjoyable are the splendid views from the windows. The public rooms look over the gardens, with their leafy avenues, canals and fountains, while the more intimate queen's apartments look into Wren's lavish Fountain Court.

## THE PALACE GARDENS

Like the palace, the gardens are in a mixture of styles. To the south, between the River Thames and the palace, is the Privy Garden, designed for the exclusive use of the royal family and separated from the river by Tijou's handsome wrought-iron screen. Here archaeologists have unearthed the formal beds and pathways that were laid out as a Dutch garden during the reign of William III. The shrubbery that grew here in the 19th century is now being cleared so that the late-17th century garden can be recreated.

Near by is Henry VIII's Pond Garden and an Elizabethan Knot Garden of aromatic herbs. The famous Great Vine grows near the Banqueting House. Planted in 1768, it still produces Black Hamburg grapes, which are on sale in season. To the north of the palace are the Wilderness, the Laburnum Walk and the well-trodden Maze, which was planted in 1714 during the reign of Queen Anne.

25

OPPOSITE *The richly decorated King's Staircase forms part of Sir Christopher Wren's rebuilding of the State Apartments in the 17th century*

LEFT *In contrast with the magnificence of the palace and its formal gardens, these colourful borders have a lovely cottage-garden style*

# *The Royal Botanic Gardens*

T HE GARDENS AT KEW ARE SUPERB AT ANY TIME OF YEAR. Even in the grey depths of winter, the Victorian glasshouses are full of luxuriant tropical growth, while spring and early summer bring massed bulbs, frothing groves of Japanese cherries and magnolias or swathes of colourful azaleas and rhododendrons. There are plants here from every corner of the globe, and to visit the gardens is to embark on a voyage through desert, swamp and rainforest.

## RESEARCH AND DISCOVERY

The gardens were created by combining two royal estates in 1772. Under the patronage of George III they developed into one of the world's foremost centres of horticultural research. The credit for this was largely due to Sir Joseph Banks, who became the king's adviser shortly after returning from a voyage round the world with Captain Cook on board the

*Kew's glasshouses, with their luxuriant specimens, are a year-round attraction — and wonderful places to be when all outside is cold and damp*

*Kew's glasshouses are as famous as the gardens themselves, and the Temperate House was the largest greenhouse in the world on its completion in 1899*

The magnificent Palm House was the first glasshouse to be built at Kew and, as its name suggests, it contains palm trees from all over the world

### INDIGENOUS PLANTS

◆

British native wild flowers are the theme at Queen Charlotte's Cottage Gardens, a peaceful spot on the south-western fringes of the site. George III's queen had a rustic 'cottage' built here in the 1770s, and the area around it is now a woodland nature reserve, in accordance with the wishes of Queen Victoria. A delightful haven at any time, this garden is particularly beautiful in May, when carpets of bluebells bloom here.

*Endeavour*. During this expedition Banks had recorded a huge number of hitherto unknown plants, which he now brought to Britain for the first time, growing them at Kew to assess their value, either as ornamental plants or as sources of food or medicines. The early botanic garden occupied a small part of the total area; the rest was landscaped by Lancelot 'Capability' Brown (his lake and Rhododendron Dell remain) and dotted with fanciful buildings for the amusement of courtly visitors: of these, the oldest is the ten-storey pagoda, towering at the southernmost end of the garden. It was built in 1761–2, to the designs of William Chambers.

### KEW'S GLASSHOUSES

Kew began to change after 1841, when the gardens were handed over to the State and several greenhouses were added. The earliest is the curvaceous Palm House, which was designed by Decimus Burton and built of wrought iron and glass, with techniques borrowed from shipbuilding. It opened in 1848 and was restored during the 1980s. In front of the Palm House are the Queen's Beasts, heraldic animals carved for the coronation of Elizabeth II in 1953. In the nearby Waterlily House (1852), the giant Amazonian lily sports leaves up to 6½ft (2m) across.

The next to be built was the Temperate House, also by Decimus Burton, beginning in 1859; by the time it was completed, 40 years later, it was the world's largest greenhouse. It has an elevated gallery from which to enjoy views of brightly coloured plants, including the Chilean wine palm, planted in 1846 and now claimed to be the largest greenhouse plant in existence.

A more recent addition is the Princess of Wales Conservatory opened in 1987, and much of it is below ground level (for insulation) and lit by a series of low, tent-like glass roofs. Computer controls simulate a number of different environments in the one building, so that visitors pass from arid desert at one end to the orchid-filled tropics at the other. Each climate zone has its own weird and wonderful plants, from the stone-like lithops of the dry regions to the carnivorous pitcher plants of the Asian rainforests.

### KEW VILLAGE

The main gate to the Royal Botanical Gardens is on Kew Green, an immaculate triangle of grass where long, lazy games of cricket are played on summer Sundays against a backdrop of late Georgian buildings, originally constructed for members of George III's court. St Anne's Church, built of yellow brick in 1714, stands on the southern edge of the green and is a quirky, attractive building with an octagonal cupola and Venetian-style windows. Thomas Gainsborough,

*Close to the Palm House is the Waterlily House, where species include the giant Amazonian lily*

the artist, is buried in the churchyard and two former directors of Kew Gardens, William and Joseph Hooker (father and son), both have unusual but appropriate memorials of porcelain decorated with ferns and flowers.

Kew Palace, a modest brick mansion also known as the Dutch House, was built by Samuel Fortrey (of Dutch descent) in 1631 and used by the royal family from the 1720s. George III, Queen Charlotte and their 15-strong brood spent much time here, and Queen Charlotte died here in 1818. The house, furnished in 18th-century style, has a small formal garden.

### KEW BRIDGE STEAM MUSEUM

◆

On the opposite bank of the Thames from Kew Gardens is the Kew Bridge Steam Museum, which houses several giant steam engines that once pumped millions of gallons of fresh water a day to supply the needs of West London. Steam-powered boats, lorries and traction engines are also on display, as well as a Victorian machine shop and forge, and London's only steam narrow-gauge railway.

*TOP The 1980s Princess of Wales Conservatories, with their low-line roofscape, provide an attractive contrast to the older glasshouses*

*The gardens and glasshouses at Kew are a centre for scientific study as well as providing the opportunity to see plants from all over the world*

# Richmond upon Thames

*RIGHT Richmond's riverside walk takes in many of its finest buildings and architectural features, as well as the fine views across the Thames*

*BELOW The view from the summit of Richmond Hill takes in this beautifully wooded curve of the wide River Thames and one of its islands*

HIS RIVERSIDE VILLAGE HAS MANY ATTRACTIONS, including the Green, an open space surrounded by 17th- and 18th-century houses, and the Little Green, with its late Victorian Richmond Theatre and the Orange Tree theatre pub, venues for the Richmond Festival in June and July. South of the green, the four houses on Maids of Honour Row were built in 1724 for the ladies-in-waiting of the Princess of Wales. Behind this row, in Old Palace Yard, is the gatehouse of Richmond Palace, most of which was demolished by Parliamentarians after the execution of Charles I.

Another notable landmark is the medieval Church of St Peter. Rebuilt in the 16th century and subsequently extended, its features include a 17th-century brick tower, pre-Victorian interior and a notable monument to George Cole (died 1624), his wife and grandson, including their effigies. George Vancouver, the navigator and colleague of Captain James Cook, is buried in the churchyard.

32

*Richmond Park is a vast tract of
natural countryside with a large herd
of deer, which are not nearly as timid
as their truly wild counterparts*

## RICHMOND RIVERSIDE

Charming little alleys full of antiques shops and boutiques lead south to the Thames, which is spanned here by Richmond Bridge. To the north of the bridge is Richmond Riverside, a group of 20 buildings in classical style, arranged around four courtyards. Only recently completed, the development is the work of Quinlan Terry, an architect who passionately believes in classical values.

Quinlan Terry's classical design for these buildings has proved surprisingly controversial. Many inhabitants of Richmond consider them to be a pleasing addition to their handsome riverfront, and a fine complement to the bridge. Other architects, however, accuse Terry of being populist and backward-looking. They also maintain that the development is dishonest, because behind the classical porticos and façades lie ordinary, steel-framed offices. It is an argument which is likely to continue for some time.

A footpath leads south under Richmond Bridge, following the course of the Thames to Ham House and offering delightful views across the river and towards Marble Hill House. This magnificent Palladian villa, built in the 1720s, can be reached by foot passengers via a ferry.

### RICHMOND BRIDGE

◆

Dating from 1777, Richmond Bridge holds the distinction of being the oldest in London — all the other bridges were rebuilt at some stage in the 18th and 19th centuries to cope with ever-increasing traffic, but Richmond's elegant five-arch bridge survives in its original form. The design itself is even older — the architect, James Paine, used as his model a bridge designed for the northern Italian town of Vicenza by the great 16th-century architect Palladio.

*This painting of Richmond Bridge by Myles Birket Foster (1825-99) can be seen at the Guildhall Art Gallery in the City of London*

## RICHMOND PARK

This large area of open space between Richmond and Kingston-upon-Thames has royal connections dating back at least to Edward I, when the area was known as the manor of Sheen. The park was enclosed by Charles I in 1637 as a royal hunting ground, and red and fallow deer still wander freely around the grassland, which is dotted with oak trees (some of which are over 600 years old) and man-made ponds. For garden lovers, the Isabella Plantation, towards the southern tip of the park, is spectacular in late spring, when the azaleas and rhododendrons are in full bloom, and has many unusual and attractive flowering trees. The two Pen Ponds in the centre of Richmond Park were created in the mid-18th century from streams within the park. Designated a Site of Special Scientific Interest, the park is also home to a number of historical buildings, including Pembroke Lodge, Richmond Gate, Sudbrook Park and White Lodge. The soaring steeple of the splendid Victorian Gothic Church of St Matthias is a landmark for miles around.

Started by George I in 1727, White Lodge has been home to a variety of royals, including the Duke and Duchess of Teck, parents of Queen Mary. King George V and Queen Mary lived here when they were the Duke and Duchess of York, and Edward VIII was born here in 1894. George VI and Queen Elizabeth lived here briefly, also as Duke and Duchess of York, with their two daughters, the Princesses Elizabeth (now Queen Elizabeth II) and Margaret. The house is now occupied by the Royal Ballet School.

# Chiswick

Sir Michael Redgrave and his now equally famous thespian family were among the residents of the fine riverside houses of Chiswick Mall

CENTRE Only Chiswick House survives from three mansions beside the river; its grand entrance is a fitting introduction to the delights within

**A**LTHOUGH CHISWICK HAS BECOME SOMETHING OF A victim of traffic, thundering along the Great West Road to reach the M4 motorway, visitors venturing from the main road find the delightful backwater which, in the 18th and 19th centuries, attracted artists such as Hogarth to make their homes here. And it was in Chiswick that Lord Burlington chose to build Chiswick House, the most perfect example of a Palladian country villa in England.

## THE HOUSES OF CHISWICK MALL

A walk along Chiswick Mall – the Upper and Lower Mall – reveals some of London's finest 18th-century houses, which reflect the wealth of their original owners, able to afford that rare commodity in London – uninterrupted views of the Thames and gardens that sweep down to the water's edge.

One of the best of these buildings is Walpole House, a rare example of Restoration period architecture, built around 1700 for Barbara Villiers, Duchess of Cleveland, who was one of Charles II's mistresses. In the 19th century it served as a school, said to be the inspiration for Miss Pinkerton's Academy for Young Ladies in Thackeray's *Vanity Fair*. Another building of note is Kelmscott House, on the Upper Mall. From 1878 to 1896 it was the home of William Morris, and is named after his country house in Oxfordshire. It was at the nearby Sussex House that Morris set up the Kelmscott Press to produce beautifully hand-illustrated books.

Along from the Mall, in Church Street, St Nicholas Church is the burial place of several famous artists and architects, including Hogarth, William Kent, Colen Campbell and James McNeill Whistler.

## CHISWICK HOUSE

Chiswick House was one of the first Palladian buidings in England. This delightful villa was built in 1725–9 by the Earl of Burlington, patron of the arts and accomplished architect, not as a residence but for entertaining and as a 'temple to the arts', taking inspiration from Palladio's Villa Capra, near Vicenza in northern Italy. The ground floor rooms, designed

## HOGARTH'S HOUSE

◆

To the north of Chiswick House stands Hogarth's House, nowadays close to a busy traffic roundabout, but the scene was very different when the 'little country box by the Thames' stood in open fields. Hogarth used it as his summer residence between 1749 and 1764 and the simple rooms are hung with copies of his satirical engravings, including the famous *Marriage à la Mode* of 1745 and *The Rake's Progress* of 1735. In the tiny garden there is an ancient mulberry tree, under which Hogarth used to sit, and it survives and bears fruit despite having been hit both by lightning and a World War II bomb, not to mention the traffic pollution.

*ABOVE AND ABOVE LEFT* The charming home of William Hogarth, champion of English art and founder of the forerunner of the Royal Academy

35

as private apartments, are relatively plain, but the upper floor is richly decorated with gilded cherubs, swags and scrolls, statues of classical deities and ceiling paintings by William Kent. Lord Burlington designed the house with architect Colen Campbell, whilst the interior and the classical-style gardens are by Kent. The house was owned by the Dukes of Devonshire, Burlington's descendants, until the 1890s, when it was converted into a private lunatic asylum.

The main east front has an elaborate double staircase leading to the two-storey portico, unlike any Palladian prototype. Flanking the staircase are fine statues carved by Rysbrack around 1730, representing Palladio and Inigo Jones, the English architect who did so much to introduce the ideals of classical architecture to England. Another homage to Inigo Jones are the obelisks on the roof around the central dome. These are, in fact, disguised chimneys, copied from designs made by Jones for the Queen's House at Greenwich, as are some of the magnificent chimney pieces inside the villa.

The garden provides a romantic setting. Although Italian in style, complete with temples, statues and obelisks, it marks a departure from the geometric form of Renaissance gardens, forming an idealised version of the Roman Campagna.

# Kensington Palace

*In front of the rather plain exterior, the superb entrance gates give an indication of the artistry to be found within the palace's State Apartments*

## LEIGHTON HOUSE
◆

Leighton House Art Gallery and Museum occupy the house designed for the artist Lord Leighton in the 1860s, and where he lived until his death in 1896. The house features sumptuous Victorian interiors, paintings by Leighton, Watts, Millais, Burne-Jones, sculpture by Hamo Thornycroft and others, an Arab Hall and Islamic tiles.

NTIL RECENTLY, KENSINGTON PALACE WAS THE ONLY royal palace in London open to the public. Queen Victoria, who was born here in 1819, decided that the State Apartments should be opened in 1889, on her 70th birthday.

Though it is no longer the residence of the monarch, several members of the present royal family still have apartments here, including Princess Margaret, Prince and Princess Michael of Kent and the Duke and Duchess of Gloucester – visitors sometimes catch a fleeting glimpse as they depart in their limousines.

## A ROYAL RETREAT

Architecturally it is surprisingly modest, more a like country house than a palace in scale and appearance, although the interiors are more sumptuous and the surrounding gardens are a great delight. It was the asthmatic William III who first set up home here, in 1689, escaping from the damp and smoke of St James's to the cleaner air and rural environment of Hyde Park. He purchased the existing house, built in 1605, and had it enlarged by Sir Christopher Wren in the 1690s. It was further extended, under George I, by William Kent in the 1720s, and the result is a roughly rectangular brick building which is arranged around three courtyards.

Visitors entering through the garden door are greeted by the simple Queen's Staircase, in mellow oak, leading to Queen Mary's Gallery. This panelled room is hung with royal portraits and Kneller's forceful picture of Peter the Great of Russia, painted when the Tsar visited England to study London's dockyards in 1698. From here, there is a series of smaller private apartments, decorated with 17th-century furnishings and pictures, including the State Bed, in Queen Mary's Bedchamber, complete with its original hangings.

## THE STATE APARTMENTS

The suite of State Apartments, though naturally less intimate, is far more striking. Italianate in style, the rooms feature magnificent ceiling paintings by William Kent. The first room, the Privy Chamber, is painted with the figure of

Mars (wearing the Order of the Garter) symbolising the military prowess of George I, and of Minerva, goddess of wisdom, accompanied by figures representing the Sciences and the Arts. The central roundel in the Presence Chamber shows Apollo in his chariot. A door leads off this room to the King's Grand Staircase, with its scrolly wrought-ironwork by Jean Tijou, and Kent's *trompe-l'œil* wall painting of a gallery crowded with figures, many of them representing George I's courtiers and servants. One of them, known as Peter the Wild Boy, was discovered living like a wild animal in a forest near Hanover and brought to England as a freak curiosity, though he rapidly adapted to the ways of the royal court.

Next is the King's Gallery, with its ceiling paintings of the adventures of Ulysses, a room which is used to display works of art from the Royal Collection. A curiosity here is the wind direction dial above the fireplace, which is turned by a weathervane on the roof. Through an ante-room is Queen Victoria's bedroom, where a painting illustrates the Queen's marriage to Prince Albert in 1840.

The King's Drawing Room beyond enjoys superb views over Kensington Gardens and is followed by the Council Chamber, which exhibits pictures and objects associated with Prince Albert's great project, the Great Exhibition of 1851.

Finally comes the most magnificent of all the State Apartments, the Cupola Room, with its pillars, figures of Greek and Roman deities and busts of Roman emperors and ancient philosophers.

## THE COURT DRESS COLLECTION

Downstairs is the excellent Court Dress Collection, with a series of tableaux showing the type of clothing that soldiers, diplomats, colonial and civil servants would have been expected to wear at official court receptions right up to recent times. However, the famous wedding dress worn by the Princess of Wales at her marriage to Prince Charles has been banished from display since the couple's separation.

## KENSINGTON PALACE GARDENS

William III was a keen gardener and lavished much affection on the garden he had laid out in Dutch style immediately around Kensington Palace. This original garden has been superceded by a pretty sunken garden, made in 1909, with an alley of pleached lime trees on three sides, and with flower beds framing the central lily pond. The fourth side of the garden is closed by the red-brick orangery of 1704. Facing south to catch the sun, this is where Queen Anne used to take tea, as visitors still can – part of the orangery serves as a restaurant. Beyond lies Kensington Gardens.

## KENSINGTON GARDENS

Kensington Gardens is adjacent to Hyde Park, the boundary marked by the carriageway that runs from Alexandra Gate in the south, over the Serpentine Bridge, and up to the Victoria Gate in the north. The division is almost imperceptible, but the differing character of the two parks is very apparent.

Kensington Gardens is relatively quiet and surprisingly rich in wildlife – herons and grebes inhabit the willow-fringed Long Water to the north of the Serpentine Bridge.

The two parks escaped being developed during the great expansion of London in the 18th century because the land belonged to the Crown. Henry VIII had seized it from the monks of Westminster Abbey at the Dissolution of the Monasteries and had turned it into a huge royal hunting ground. Later it was opened to 'respectably dressed people' and became a favourite resort of Pepys, among others.

*This gleaming statue of Queen Victoria stands outside her former home, featuring the intriguing and eye-catching Grand Staircase, opposite*

39

*Generations of young visitors to Kensington Gardens have been enchanted by this statue of Peter Pan, the boy who never grew up*

### NEVER NEVER LAND

◆

One of the most famous features of Kensington Gardens is the delightful statue of Peter Pan (1912) by George Frampton, which commemorates the hero of J M Barrie's play for children, written in 1904, while the playground is the site of the Elfin Oak, a tree trunk carved by Ivor Innes in 1928 with elves, foxes, frogs, rabbits and secret doorways.

# The Victoria & Albert Museum

*T*HE V & A, AS IT IS AFFECTIONATELY KNOWN, IS THE world's finest museum of decorative arts, a storehouse of treasures so diverse as to defy general description. It contains over 4 million objects from every age and nation, and though in broad terms the collection covers 'applied art', this description does not do any justice to the immense diversity, eclecticism and idiosyncracy of its material. The collections include superb examples of textiles from around the world, architectural fragments from French châteaux, Indian chess sets, medieval reliquaries and a bed so famous that it featured in the plays of Shakespeare and Ben Jonson.

## THE EARLY YEARS

The museum is, of course, named after Queen Victoria and her consort, who were directly responsible for its existence. It was a natural progression from the immensely successful Great Exhibition of 1851, which was a celebration of the arts,

*The Nehru Gallery of Indian Art forms just part of a vast Asian collection, and houses some of the finest examples from the region*

crafts and industrial products of the British Empire. Prince Albert, the driving force behind the exhibition, wanted this to be a permanent collection displaying the best examples of commercial art and design as a source of inspiration to future generations. The first museum on the site was called the

Road façade were among the last parts to be built, and Queen Victoria laid the foundation stone in 1899 – her last public engagement in London. The building was completed in 1909. The entrance is topped by a great cupola, modelled on the Queen's imperial crown, and statues of Victoria and Albert preside over the entrance.

## AROUND THE MUSEUM

The museum is so vast that you cannot possibly see everything in a single visit. Those with a particular interest usually select one or two rooms to study in detail, but it is great fun just to wander around the maze of galleries, being in turn surprised and delighted by the discoveries along the way. Some galleries have been remodelled with the help of commercial sponsorship, and give a good flavour of the museum. From the main hall, the central corridor houses medieval art, one of the best collections of its kind in the world, ranging from 5th-century ivories to Saxon goldwork and Carolingian gospel bindings.

Among many other highlights are the world's greatest collection of paintings by John Constable and the national collection of watercolours, the Raphael Cartoons, the Dress Court, showing fashion since 1500, and the Jewellery Gallery, which includes the Russion crown jewels. There is a magnificent collection of Renaissance and Victorian sculpture and a superb Asian collection, spread among the Toshiba Gallery of Japanese Art, the Nehru Gallery of Indian Art and the T T Tsui Gallery of Chinese Art. The 20th-century Galleries include the 'Now Room', with changing exhibitions of the very latest in art and design.

Applied art that is an integral part of the building can be seen in the Morris, Gamble and Poynter rooms. Originally the museum tea-rooms and restaurant, they retain their Minton tilework, William Morris furnishings and Burne-Jones stained glass.

41

*The magnificent and extensive façade of the V & A, whose current building was designed by Sir Aston Webb*

Museum of Manufactures; it later became the Museum of Ornamental Art before acquiring its present name. As the collection grew, the building was extended; today it has over 7 miles (11km) of gallery space on its six floors, arranged around a central courtyard. The main entrance and Cromwell

### FAVOURITE EXHIBITS

◆

The Great Bed of Ware is one of the V & A's most celebrated exhibits, partly because of its prodigious size (10ft/3m wide and nearly 13ft/4m long), but also because of its great age – it was made around 1590 – not to mention its extravagant carved, painted and inlaid decoration. Another celebrated curiosity is Tippoo's Tiger, a large model tiger in the Nehru Gallery of Indian art, which is shown in the act of eating a British army officer. Made in 1790 for the Tippoo Sahib of Mysore, the model incorporates a small organ that imitates the groans of the tiger's victim.

# The Natural History Museum

*ABOVE The main entrance is a wonder to behold, with its subtle colouring and intricate carving, while below, the diplodocus skeleton is a familiar sight to millions of visitors*

HERE IS NO MISTAKING THE PURPOSE OF THIS magnificent building – its elaborate exterior incorporates relief mouldings of animals, birds, insects and fish, running the whole length of the 676ft (206m) façade, with representations of living species to the left of the entrance and extinct ones to the right.

The nucleus of the collections here were the specimens collected by Sir Hans Sloane, which were formerly displayed at the British Museum, but by 1860 the collections had expanded so much that the need for a separate national Natural History museum could no longer be ignored. All this coincided with a time when the subject of natural history was at the forefront of popular (and usually heated) debate. Three years earlier Charles Darwin had published *The Origin of Species,* which set supporters of his evolutionary theories at loggerheads with those sceptics who insisted on the Biblical version of the Creation.

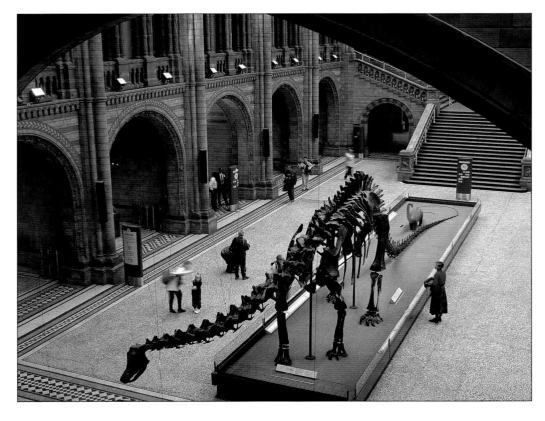

## THE LIFE GALLERIES

The Life Galleries explore all aspects of human, animal and plant life. Dinosaurs have been extinct for about 65 million years, but they still hold tremendous fascinating for us. The Central Hall contains a huge plaster-cast skeleton of a 150 million-year-old *Diplodocus carnegii,* excavated in Wyoming. It was one of the largest land animals ever to have roamed the earth and is a splendid introduction to the main dinosaur exhibition off to the left, which attempts to explain the life and death of these creatures. Among the most popular exhibits is Mammals, its most prominent feature a gigantic life-size model of a blue whale. The lives of hundreds of

of any museum, and range from the beautiful etchings on slate walls of the solar system and night sky to exciting recreations of an earthquake and erupting volcano. One of Britain's longest escalators transports visitors from the introductory exhibits on the ground floor up to the second floor galleries. The Power Within brings to life the terrifying natural phenomena of forces deep within the earth. The earthquake experience is kept within the bounds of safety, but shows what it is like to feel the earth tremor. It takes place in a recreation of the supermarket in Japan which suffered that fate a few years ago, complete with actual footage from the store's security cameras.

In another alarming re-creation, visitors walk beneath a volcano, see what happens during an eruption and experience an emergency evacuation. Both of these exhibits are accompanied by eye-witness accounts and video footage of actual events. The Restless Surface exhibition tells the story of how the surface of the earth is shaped and reshaped by the elements, including the causes and effects of tidal waves, tornados, hurricanes, landslides and avalanches. Visitors can recreate the wind's sand-blasting action on rock, experiment with gravity and discover how a single piece of rock can give up evidence of a billion years of change.

## VISIONS OF EARTH

The ground floor of the Earth Galleries illustrates our understanding of the earth in a dramatic and artistic way. Slate walls flanking the entrance are beautifully etched with the solar system and night sky, and portholes cut out of the wall have displays of specimens, such as crystals and a piece of moon rock, which show the diversity of the earth's history and forms. A series of sculptures traces our changing perceptions of the earth in the forms of Atlas, Medusa, Cyclops, a female scientist and an astronaut, progressing from ancient mythology, through scientific discovery (and sexual equality) to the time when we could travel into space and look back on the earth from afar.

### THE GIANT SEQUOIA TREE
◆

One of the most intriguing exhibits in the Natural History Museum is a section through a giant sequoia tree (*Sequoiadendron giganteum*) displayed on the stairs to the second floor of the Life Galleries. The tree was cut down in 1892, by which time it was 275ft (84m) tall and measured 45ft (15m) round the girth. A tree-ring count indicates that it was 1,335 years old when felled, having started its life in California in AD 557.

CENTRE *The grounds of the museum include a wildlife garden, which was completed in 1995*

43

*The main building of the Natural History Museum complex shows classic lines and great symmetry*

animals, including the Tasmanian devil, dolphins, elephants and tigers, are revealed here. At the opposite end of the scale is the Creepy Crawlies exhibition, which attempts to convince us that insects, spiders, crabs and their relatives really are important to humans. It includes an exhibition house, within which lurk all manner of uninvited guests – seek them out to discover whether they are friend or foe.

## THE EARTH GALLERIES

An exciting development at the museum is the Earth Galleries, housed in the former Geological Museum. These displays here are among the most innovative and imaginative

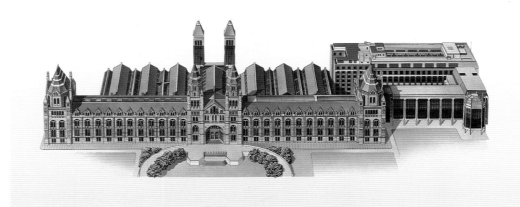

# The Science Museum

*CENTRE The museum has a vast array of railway engines, motor cars and other forms of transport*

*BELOW The exploration of space is one of the most popular and informative exhibits on display*

INCE THE DAYS WHEN THE INDUSTRIAL REVOLUTION thrust the world into a new era, the progress of science and technology has been hurtling forward at ever-increasing speed. This museum, founded to celebrate the Industrial Revolution, has kept pace with that progress and is now one of the most exciting museums in London. If the word 'museum' still conjures up an image of dusty displays in an atmosphere of hushed respect for the past, a visit to the Science Museum will soon dispel it. Parts of it resemble nothing so much as a huge, noisy playground, while elsewhere are gleaming reminders of past achievements and glimpses of future possibilities.

## MOTIVE POWER

The museum advocates a policy of entertaining as well as informing, and even the most technophobic visitor will find something of interest. Few could fail to be fascinated by the immensely long Foucault Pendulum, whose movement demonstrates the Earth's rotation.

The galleries devoted to early motoring and the age of steam are also a big attraction. Vehicles here include a Benz three-wheeler motor car of 1888 and a 1904 Rolls Royce, while the pioneering days of the railways are represented by the world's oldest steam locomotive, *Puffing Billy* (1813) and

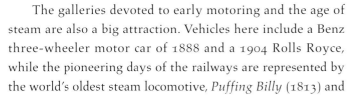

## DOMESTIC AND MEDICAL SCIENCE
◆

The lower ground floor features reconstructions of a Victorian bathroom and kitchen, a collection of domestic appliances and the Bryant & May collection of matches. Even food has moved on from the days when you would just catch something, or dig it up, and eat it.

The Wellcome Museum of the History of Medicine displays early medical instruments resembling instruments of torture, and interesting historical items, such as Napoleon's toothbrush and Florence Nightingale's moccasins.

George Stephenson's *Rocket*, which won the Rainhill Trials of 1829. Exhibits from the national Aeronautic Collection include early aircraft, such as Alcock and Brown's Vickers-Vimy (1919), the first to cross the Atlantic, and the Gipsy Moth, in which Amy Johnson flew to Australia in 1930.

Space exploration is also covered extensively, and exhibits include the Apollo 10 capsule which took astronauts round the Moon for the first time in May 1969, and a recreation of a futuristic moon-base.

*The plasma ball launch pad holds a fascination for visitors of all ages*

## HANDS-ON TECHNOLOGY

◆

Children, and most adults, love the hands-on exhibits and try-it-yourself experiments of the Launch Pad Gallery, which is designed to stimulate enquiring minds with working models. At the turn of a handle, or the push of a knob, various exhibits are set in motion, light up, rotate or make noises. Even more popular is the second-floor gallery, where the displays are devoted to computers and silicon-chip technology.

The computer-generated graphics demonstrated here make the very first photographs, taken by W H Fox Talbot in 1835, look primitive – but his cameras, displayed on the third floor, are beautiful examples of craftsmanship, as is the microscope near by, made by George Adams around 1770 for George III.

## ART, SCIENCE AND HISTORY

Art and science are so often regarded as incompatible, but some of the Science Museum's exhibits bridge that gulf. *Coalbrookdale by Night* by P J de Loutherbourg (1801) is a dramatic representation of the fiery furnaces that lit up the skies of the birthplace of the Industrial Revolution, appropriately and arrestingly displayed in the Iron and Steel Gallery. The intricate Orrery of 1716, made for and named after the Earl of Orrery, is a working model of the solar system, and nature's artistry is also demonstrated by the model of the DNA spiral on the second floor.

Among displays at the cutting edge of technology are also some ancient exhibits, the oldest being the clock mechanism from Wells Cathedral, still working after some 600 years. Important industrial history is represented by Arkwright's original spinning machine of 1769, one of the pioneering inventions that sparked the Industrial Revolution, with its far-reaching implications for the way we live today.

# Chelsea and Knightsbridge

46

THE ROYAL BOROUGH OF KENSINGTON AND CHELSEA encompasses some of the most stylish and innovative areas of London. The area is the epitome of chic, full of elegant houses and gardens and famed for its shops around the King's Road, the Sloane Street area and Brompton Road, site of that most famous of shops – Harrods.

## HARRODS

Harrods has become a legend among stores. Its Latin motto, *Omnia, omnibus, ubique* – everything, for everyone, everywhere – is no empty slogan, for Harrods sells just about everything and its customers come from all over the world.

The store is so vast that it publishes a store guide to help customers find their way around. It also has an information desk near the entrance to offer general assistance and details of product demonstrations, special exhibitions and author signings. The distinctive terracotta-clad five-storey building, which is illuminated at night, occupies an entire block in Brompton Road, stretching from Hans Crescent to Hans Road, and dates from the early 1900s. It houses over 230 departments, run by over 4,000 staff, and an average day's takings will exceed £1 million. On one happy day in 1986 a grand total of £6 million was handed over the counters.

The name of Harrods has also become synonymous with quality, and there are certainly many very exclusive departments with items at staggering prices, but there are ordinary everyday goods too, which sell here for ordinary prices. The January sales are always guaranteed to offer remarkable bargains to determined shoppers who can cope with the crowds and the crush.

On the ground floor the splendid food halls are a major attraction, where the décor is as delectable as the unbelievable range of quality foods on display. Above the fish, meat and poultry halls are wonderful tiled ceilings depicting The Hunt which were made by W J Neatley in 1902. There are equally lavish art deco ceramics elsewhere in the store – most notably in the men's hairdressing rooms and the ladies lavatory. The upper floors include such delights for children as the pet shop and Toy Kingdom, and there are several restaurants.

## THE HISTORY OF HARRODS

The Harrods of today is a far cry from the small grocery store which was founded by Charles Henry Harrod in 1849. In the 1860s, Charles Henry's son, Charles Digby, took over the store and proceeded to build it up into a giant department store before his retirement in 1891. In 1898 Harrods installed London's first escalator to transport its customers to the upper floors (where smelling salts and brandy were waiting to revive those of a nervous disposition). The House of Fraser took over the store in 1959, but since 1986 it has been run by the Egyptian-born al Fayed brothers.

## CHELSEA ROYAL HOSPITAL

Chelsea Pensioners, as they are popularly known, are a resplendent sight in their scarlet or dark blue uniforms, which hark back to the founding of the hospital by Charles II in 1682 as a home for veteran and invalid soldiers.

The magnificent building was designed by Sir Christopher Wren, who took his inspiration from the Hôtel des Invalides in Paris, and as well as housing over 400 old soldiers, it contains a museum of medals, uniforms, photographs and other items connected with its history. Wren's work can be seen at its finest in the Figure Court and the Chapel. Chelsea's Royal Avenue is part of a road designed by Wren to link the Royal Hospital with Kensington Palace. The road was never finished, but the section that remains was completed in 1694 (the terraces of houses which line the road date from the 19th century).

The hospital has attractive grounds running down to the Chelsea Embankment on the River Thames. They contain an 1850s obelisk commemorating the Battle of Chillianwallah (1849) in the Second Sikh War.

Adjacent to, and owned by, the Royal Hospital are the delightful Ranelagh Gardens. In the 18th century these were the Ranelagh Pleasure Gardens, a much favoured venue for the nobility to indulge in music, opera, gambling, dancing and masquerades. Towards the end of the century, these events seemed to lose their appeal and eventually the gardens closed in 1804. The Hospital then added the gardens to their

existing grounds. The summer house was designed by Sir John Soane and, at the corner of the Chelsea Embankment and Chelsea Bridge Road, is a monument to the Carabineers who fought in the Boer War. The most famous event held in the gardens these days is the Chelsea Flower Show, which is the highlight of the horticultural year. All the major growers have stands and display gardens are created specially for the event. At the end of the final day, exhibits are sold to the public at very reasonable prices.

## OAK APPLE DAY

The Chelsea Pensioners honour their founder Charles II each year on 29th May, on the anniversary of his escape after the Battle of Worcester in 1651. There is a colourful parade, and a statue of Charles II by Grinling Gibbons is decked with oak branches as a reminder that his escape was facilitated by hiding in an oak tree on the Boscobel estate.

## ROYAL HOSPITAL GRAVEYARD

There is a saying that goes 'old soldiers never die…' This may not be strictly true, but there were four inhabitants of the Royal Hospital who seemed to be putting off the moment for as long as possible. In the small graveyard to the east their graves list their ages as being from 107 to 112. One of the quartet, William Hiseland, married when he was over 100. Also buried in here is Hannah Snell, who died in 1792 having served in both the army and navy as a man.

47

## CHELSEA PHYSIC GARDEN

◆

This garden off Royal Hospital Road was founded in the 1670s for research into medicinal and useful plants. Still a research centre, it features rare and notable trees and plants and a 1770s rock garden – one of Europe's earliest. It also contains a statue by Rysbrack of Sir Hans Sloane, a major benefactor.

# ·CENTRAL LONDON·

This is the heart of the capital and the nerve-centre of the country — always busy, always noisy, the place where it is all happening. Black cabs hurtle around the streets like swarms of angry beetles, and pedestrians stride purposefully along the pavements, weaving through the endless streams of traffic. It is said that London has the best taxi drivers in the world — and the worst pedestrians.

This is, of course, the seat of government, with the Houses of Parliament a splendid sight by the River Thames, and of the monarchy, whose principal residence is Buckingham Palace. This combination gives rise to many of the ceremonial events for which London is so famous, and on certain days the city streets trade the noise of traffic for the stirring sound of military bands and the clip clop of horses' hooves. The most notable of these include the Trooping the Colour ceremony in June and the State Opening of Parliament in October. The Changing of the Guard at Buckingham Palace is a daily event which always draws a crowd.

Central London is also one of the entertainment capitals of the world, and the West End is the home of a huge number of theatres, showing every kind of production. There are also music and comedy clubs and, of course, cinemas, of which the Odeon in Leicester Square is the most famous. Informal entertainment is the order of the day around Covent Garden, where street performers of all kinds entertain.

There is also the best in shopping, with exclusive shops and galleries, department stores and popular high-street chain stores. The converted market building at Covent Garden is good for arts and crafts and there are lots of fascinating little specialist shops around Soho. But, amongst all this bustle and activity are havens of tranquillity in Westminster Abbey, St James's Park and Hyde Park.

This magnificent roof towers not over a cathedral nave, but over the 19th-century Smithfield Market, London's principal wholesale meat market

# The Royal Albert Hall

IN 1867 QUEEN VICTORIA LAID THE FOUNDATION STONE of the splendid concert hall that was to be named after her beloved consort, Prince Albert. Four years later, the Royal Albert Hall opened and has been the venue for the best in classical music ever since.

The huge circular wall is composed of red brick, adorned with terracotta, including a Minton frieze illustrating the Triumphs of Art and Science. All this is surmounted by a vast dome of glass and iron. The hall was designed by Captain Francis Fowke of the Royal Engineers and built by Colonel H Y Darracott after Fowke's death in 1865. At the back of the hall is a statue of Prince Albert by Joseph Durham.

The auditorium, seating around 5,000, has a very intimate feel to it, and the tiers of boxes rising up the sides create a very picturesque sight. Modern audio techniques have been brought to bear to improve the acoustics in recent years – before that the sound tended to drift up into the dome and stay there. The hall contains one of the world's largest organs; indeed it was the largest of all when it was made by 'Father' Willis, and Bruckner played it at the opening concert.

The programme of events at the Royal Albert Hall has expanded considerably, and these days it is used for pop as well as classical concerts, and for sporting events, rallies, meetings and grand dances. However, it remains best known for the annual Sir Henry Wood Promenade Concerts, which are held daily from mid-July to mid-September. Established in the 1940s, the Proms encompass the whole range of classical music and their culmination – the Last Night of the Proms – is a joyful and noisy celebration at which the somewhat stuffy mantle of the classics is well and truly shed.

50

*OPPOSITE London is one of the great cultural centres of the world, and the Royal Albert Hall hosts one of its major musical events – The Proms*

*Flag waving and riotous renditions of patriotic songs, with full audience participation, are an integral part of the Last Night of the Proms*

# Hyde Park

*A mass of springtime daffodils bring a touch of the countryside to the formality of the monumental arches of Hyde Park Corner*

## MARBLE ARCH
◆

This triumphal arch, designed on a Roman model by John Nash in the 1820s, was moved from Buckingham Palace in 1851 not because it was too narrow for the State coaches to pass through, but to make way for new buildings. The bronze gates date from the early 20th century. The notorious Tyburn gallows was close to this spot. Pedestrianised and surrounded by traffic, its gates remain firmly shut to all but members of the royal family.

YDE PARK IS A HUGE EXPANSE OF TREES, FLOWERS AND greenery – a place of recreation and entertainment in the heart of London, with boats for hire on the Serpentine in summer, bandstand music at lunchtime in June, July and August, and occasionally fairs, concerts or fireworks parties.

Hyde Park has remained an open space throughout the capital's history, surviving initially because of the love of early monarchs for the chase. It is located west of Park Lane, east of Kensington Gardens; Bayswater Road lies on its northern boundary and Knightsbridge to the south. Central London's largest park, it extends to more than 630 acres (255 hectares) if the adjoining Kensington Gardens are included. Containing open and natural parkland with trees, birdlife and a lake and pond, the park belonged to Westminster Abbey in the Middle Ages but was taken over as a royal hunting and hawking ground by Henry VIII in 1536, when it became a Royal Park. There has been increasing access from the time of James I as it gradually turned into a pleasure park.

## THE KING'S ROAD
To the south is Rotten Row – the name is a corruption of *route du roi* (King's Road) – down which monarchs once rode on their way to hunt deer in the park. In the reign of William III and Mary II, towards the end of the 17th century, Kensington Palace became the principal royal residence. The king had to travel between the palace and St James's through the park, which was notorious for thieves, so he had the road lit with 300 oil lamps, making it the first artificially lit highway in Britain. The carriageway is now used by the Household Cavalry Brigade for exercising their horses, and at around 10.30am and noon, members of the Brigade ride to and from the Changing of the Guard ceremonies, which take place at Buckingham Palace and Horseguards.

## PARK MONUMENTS
At the western end of Piccadilly and south-eastern corner of Hyde Park is Hyde Park Corner, where traffic to and from London used to go through a tollgate; it now charges through

*Wellington Arch at Hyde Park Corner was named after the man who routed Napoleon in 1815. His London home, now a museum, is near by*

*The British countryside, complete with stately old trees, has been convincingly recreated amidst some of London's busiest streets*

an underpass and around a substantial roundabout. On the northern side is Apsley House, with its 1820s gateway to the park by Decimus Burton. In the open space in the centre of roundabout is the Wellington Arch or Constitution Arch, a triumphal arch also designed by Decimus Burton in the 1820s, surmounted by Peace driving a chariot and four horses, 1912 by Adrian Jones. Here also is a statue by Boehm in 1888 of the Duke of Wellington astride his Waterloo charger, Copenhagen. The Machine Gun Corps memorial on the same site commemorates those slain in World War I.

## THE ALBERT MEMORIAL

George Gilbert Scott's flamboyant monument to Prince Albert, husband of Queen Victoria, is a reminder of the values of the Victorian age. In the centre is Albert himself, holding the catalogue for the 1851 Great Exhibition, which he organised. Completed in 1876, the memorial is crowded with 169 portraits of painters, poets and architects. Its corners illustrate the peoples of Asia, America, Europe and Africa, while allegorical figures represent Albert's interests: Commerce, Manufacture, Engineering and Agriculture. Weather and pollution have caused serious deterioration, and protective sheeting now keeps the frost and rain at bay. Despite the huge cost, work has now begun on its restoration, which is timed for completion by the year 2000. During restoration, an excellent visitor centre is open on site, detailing the work being carried out.

## THE PEOPLE'S PARK

At Hyde Park Corner, behind Apsley House, a triple-arched screen (1828, by Decimus Burton) marks the main entrance to the park. Serpentine Road leads straight ahead to the northern shore of the Serpentine, a lake created in 1730 on the instruction of Queen Caroline, wife of George II, by damming the River Westbourne. A beautiful bridge, built in 1826 by George Rennie, spans the water. Swimming in the Serpentine is allowed at the Lido, on the opposite bank. There is also a hardy band of people, members of the Serpentine

*The Albert Memorial was designed by Sir George Gilbert Scott in the style of a medieval reliquary, and the statue of the Prince Consort is by J H Foley*

Swimming Club, who come here every day for a dip between 6 and 9am – even in the depths of winter. Near by is the Serpentine Gallery, which hosts exhibitions of 20th-century art in the summer months, and to the north of the gallery is the sculpture *Physical Energy* (1904), a powerful equestrian figure by George Frederick Watts.

55

*Serious speakers and eccentric orators alike attract attentive crowds to Speaker's Corner on Sunday mornings for guaranteed free entertainment*

### SPEAKER'S CORNER

◆

At the north-eastern edge of Hyde Park, near Marble Arch, is the site where, every Sunday morning since the 1870s, soap-box orators have harangued the crowds on issues ranging from politics and religion to vegetarianism or the evils of smoking. There have been huge gatherings here in the past, including demonstrations against nuclear armaments. According to law, anyone can speak on any topic, as long as they do not blaspheme, use obscene language, incite racial hatred or breach the peace.

# Buckingham Palace

THIS, THE ROYAL FAMILY'S PRINCIPAL RESIDENCE IN London, is located at the west end of the Mall, the ceremonial approach to it. Built by the Duke of Buckingham in the early 1700s, it was originally called Buckingham House. It was bought by George III in 1762, subsequently grandified for George IV by John Nash in the 1820s and then altered in the 1830s and 1840s by Edward Blore. The familiar present form of the east front facing the Mall is by Sir Aston Webb in 1913. Edward VII was born and died here.

The royal court has moved several times in the last 900 years – first from the City to the Palace of Westminster under Edward the Confessor in the 11th century, then to Whitehall Palace under Henry VIII in the 16th, and then to St James's Palace during the reign of Charles II. St James's remained the official residence of the sovereign throughout the 17th and 18th centuries, and it was here that the big state functions took place (foreign ambassadors are still officially accredited to 'the Court of St James's'). Even so, these cramped and ancient Tudor buildings could hardly be called palatial, and many a monarch would retire at night to the more opulent rooms of Kensington Palace.

## The Official Royal Residence

It was at Kensington Palace that Queen Victoria was born in 1819, and it remained her home until her accession to the throne in 1837. She then chose to make Buckingham Palace the official London residence of the monarch, and it has continued as such to the present day.

Against the classical backdrop of the palace's grand façade one of London's most popular events takes place, when sentries of the Guards Division in full dress uniform perform the Changing of the Guard. Spectators watch from the palace railings, with their five wrought-iron and bronze gates, decorated with cherubs and erected in 1906. An alternative vantage point is the Queen Victoria Memorial, which stands in the traffic island in front of the palace. This marble column, erected in 1911, is topped by the gilded figure of Victory, while Queen Victoria sits facing down the Mall,

*One of the most recognised sights in the world, this view of the palace sums up the popular image of London as a place of royalty and pageantry*

*ABOVE The imposing Throne Room, completed by Edward Blore for William IV, is where the Queen receives addresses on formal occasions*

accompanied by the figures of Charity, Truth and Justice. Surrounding the monument is a balustrade decorated with mermaids and bronze groups representing Peace, Prosperity, Manufacturing, Agriculture, Shipbuilding, Architecture, Painting and Mining.

### THE COURT AND THE SEASON

When the Queen is in residence at Buckingham Palace, the Royal Standard is flown from the flagpole above the central pediment. This is most likely to be between April and mid-August, when the Queen holds court in London, a period still known as 'the season'. Among aristocratic circles the season is marked by numerous social, sporting and fund-raising events, though young ladies making their first official appearances in public ('debutantes', or 'debs') are no longer 'presented' at court.

*OPPOSITE Rarely seen from the inside, the Centre Room is familiar to millions around the world for its balcony, scene of royal gatherings*

Come mid-August, the gentry heads for the country for the shooting season, and the Queen circulates between her other residences at Windsor, Sandringham and Balmoral.

### THE OPENING OF THE PALACE

◆

In 1993 the Queen announced that Buckingham Palace would open to the public for the first time in its long history – but only from mid-August to the end of September each year. The funds raised from admission charges are intended to contribute to the cost of restoring the fire damage at Windsor Castle. The very high entrance fee seems to be no deterrent, and long queues are the norm, giving an indication of the fascination that the royal lifestyle still holds.

Open all year, the Queen's Gallery at the rear of the palace is housed in a temple-like structure that was originally built as a garden conservatory. It was then converted to the palace chapel in 1893 and finally turned into an art gallery in 1962. Here you can see paintings, drawings and furniture from the vast royal collections, including works by Rubens, Rembrandt and Canaletto, as well as watercolours painted by Queen Victoria.

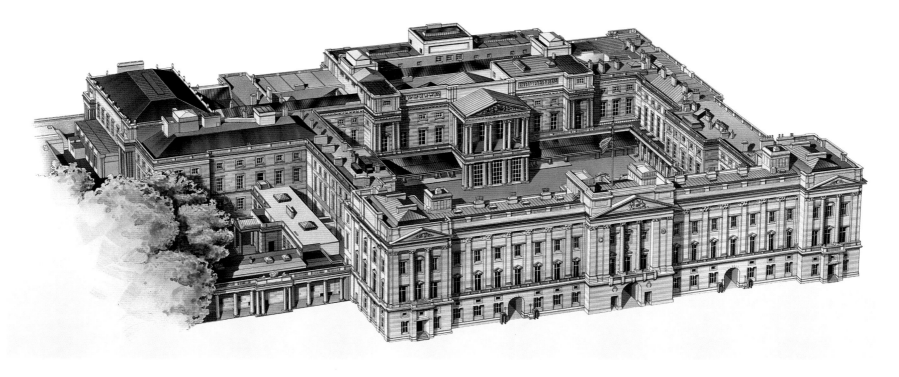

## THE ROYAL MEWS

The Royal Mews were built in 1824–5 to house the royal household's horses and coaches. Here are displayed the splendid state carriages that are used on major state occasions. They include the richly carved and gilded Gold Carriage, made for George III in 1762 and used for coronations; the Irish State Coach, bought by Queen Victoria in 1852 and used for the State Opening of Parliament; the so-called Glass State Coach, bought in 1910 and used to convey visiting dignitaries and overseas ambassadors and the open-top landau used for the weddings of the Prince and Princess of Wales in 1981 and the Duke and Duchess of York in 1986.

*ABOVE Few are privileged enough to see beyond the palace railings and façade, which conceal a huge complex of buildings around a great courtyard*

61

*LEFT The fairy-tale gold State Coach, used for coronations and jubilees, is the most famous of the collection of State Coaches in the Royal Mews*

*OPPOSITE The Music Room is used for receiving guests during State Visits, and some of the Queen's children were christened here*

# The Tate Gallery

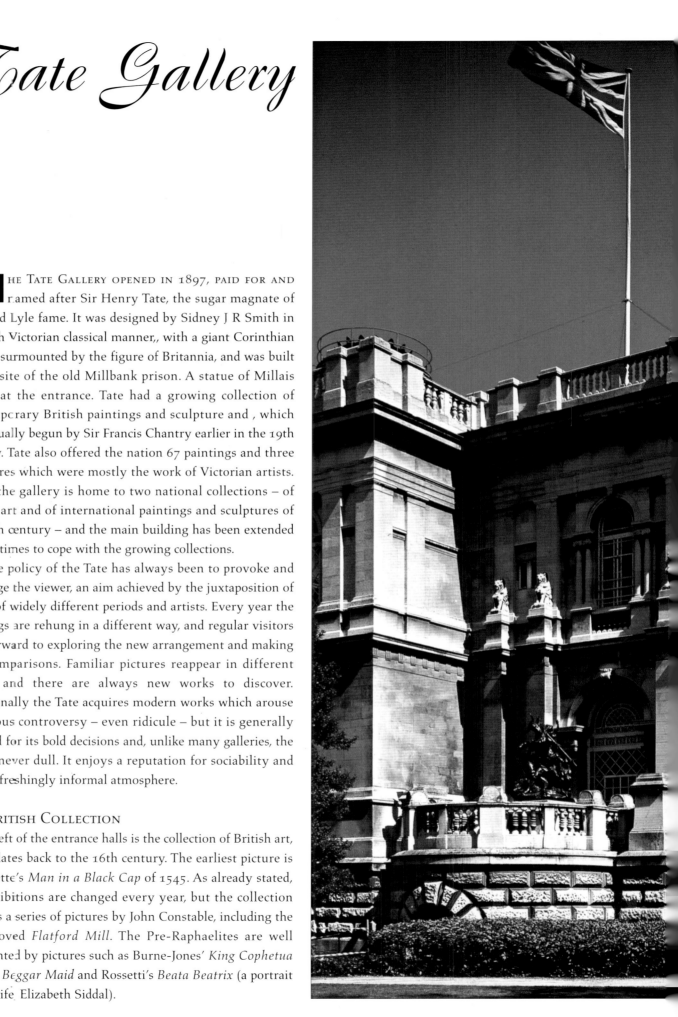

CENTRE *The Tate Gallery's neo-classical main building is on the site of a former prison – the Millbank Penitentiary*

## THE ART OF CONTROVERSY

◆

The Tate Gallery will be forever remembered for its purchase of a very expensive pile of bricks, which had the conservative press up in arms and the bricklayers of Britain in stitches!. Undeterred, the Tate recently displayed a piece entitled *Weight and Measure 1992* by the American artist Richard Serra, consisting of two huge rectangular blocks of steel, forged at great cost in Germany. It almost seems as if the Tate goes out of its way to court controversy, but it remains immensely popular, especially among art students and practising artists.

HE TATE GALLERY OPENED IN 1897, PAID FOR AND named after Sir Henry Tate, the sugar magnate of Tate and Lyle fame. It was designed by Sidney J R Smith in the high Victorian classical manner,, with a giant Corinthian portico surmounted by the figure of Britannia, and was built on the site of the old Millbank prison. A statue of Millais stands at the entrance. Tate had a growing collection of contemporary British paintings and sculpture and , which was actually begun by Sir Francis Chantry earlier in the 19th century. Tate also offered the nation 67 paintings and three sculptures which were mostly the work of Victorian artists. Today the gallery is home to two national collections – of British art and of international paintings and sculptures of the 20th century – and the main building has been extended several times to cope with the growing collections.

The policy of the Tate has always been to provoke and challenge the viewer, an aim achieved by the juxtaposition of works of widely different periods and artists. Every year the paintings are rehung in a different way, and regular visitors look forward to exploring the new arrangement and making new comparisons. Familiar pictures reappear in different places, and there are always new works to discover. Occasionally the Tate acquires modern works which arouse enormous controversy – even ridicule – but it is generally admired for its bold decisions and, unlike many galleries, the Tate is never dull. It enjoys a reputation for sociability and has a refreshingly informal atmosphere.

## THE BRITISH COLLECTION

To the left of the entrance halls is the collection of British art, which dates back to the 16th century. The earliest picture is John Bette's *Man in a Black Cap* of 1545. As already stated, the exhibitions are changed every year, but the collection contains a series of pictures by John Constable, including the much-loved *Flatford Mill*. The Pre-Raphaelites are well represented by pictures such as Burne-Jones' *King Cophetua and the Beggar Maid* and Rossetti's *Beata Beatrix* (a portrait of his wife Elizabeth Siddal).

*Left J M W Turner's oil painting of Waterloo Bridge is just one of the large collection bequeathed by the author*

## THE TURNER BEQUEST

The most recent addition was the Clore Gallery of 1987, housing the collection of paintings by J M W Turner, which the artist bequeathed to the nation upon his death in 1851 and which were formerly at the National Gallery. The bequest specified that the works should be displayed together, and they are shown here to their best advantage, with natural light doing proper justice to Turner's subtle palette. The windows give intriguing glimpses of the Thames, beside which Turner painted in his Chelsea home, and which features in many of his works.

## THE MODERN GALLERIES

This is where the more controversial works are displayed, and noisy discussion is not infrequent. The foreign collection includes representative works, with paintings by Cézanne, Matisse, Picasso, Braque, Chagall, Klee, Mondrian and Stella. There are important works by 20th-century British artists, including Stanley Spencer, Patrick Heron, Francis Bacon, John Piper and Graham Sutherland. Many of the works challenge convention, from William Blake's visionary illustrations for Dante's *The Divine Comedy* to Stanley Spencer's iconoclastic interpretations of *The Resurrection* and the work of Abstract Expressionists such as Jackson Pollock

*Above The Tate's central gallery has played host to many unusual and controversial exhibits over the years*

## OUTPOSTS

The Tate's collections are vast – the Turner Bequest alone consists of more than 20,000 works – and the gallery is keen to put a great deal more on show to the public. In order to do this, they have set up outposts of the gallery in other parts of the country. The Liverpool gallery serves the north and the one in the West Country adds a new dimension to the already artistic community of St Ives, Cornwall. The Tate is spreading to additional premises in London, too, and the modern art collection will move to a new home in the former Bankside power station near Southwark Bridge by the year 2000.

# The Houses of Parliament

*ABOVE AND LEFT The House of Lords, the chamber of hereditary and life peers, judges and bishops, is by far the more sumptuously furnished and decorated of the two chambers*

*ABOVE RIGHT The chamber of the House of Commons has become a familiar sight since the televising of parliament in session, usually a very noisy affair*

*OPPOSITE The rebuilding of the Palace of Westminster in the mid-19th century created both an impressive building and a magnificent riverscape*

THE MONUMENTAL BUILDINGS OF THE HOUSES OF Parliament are a splendid sight, especially now that the stonework has been cleaned, and the best views are undoubtedly those from the far side of Westminster Bridge, looking across the Thames to the 244m (800ft) frontage, with its symmetrically placed towers and pinnacles.

The Parliament Square façade is much more varied, stretching from the Victoria Tower to the Clock Tower, popularly known as Big Ben, though this is actually the name of the great bell inside which strikes the hour. In between lies the low roof of Westminster Hall, the oldest surviving building on the site. Inside it has a magnificent hammerbeam roof dating from 1399, but the Hall itself is much older, having been completed in 1099. There is talk of opening the Hall to the public in the near future – the plan is to make a visitor centre in the Mall, where guided tours can be booked in the mornings, but this will not happen until the new office block for MPs is completed. Meanwhile, the general public may attend debates when Parliament is sitting by queueing at the St Stephen's porch entrance.

## THE PALACE OF WESTMINSTER

Edward the Confessor built the Palace of Westminster on this site in 1049 and successive monarchs used it as their main London residence until 1529, when Henry VIII decided to move northwards to the Palace of Whitehall. Parliament (from the Old French word for a discussion or debate) first met in the Chapter House of Westminster Abbey but transferred its sittings to the vacated Palace of Westminster in 1547, where it has met ever since.

Fire destroyed most of the old Palace of Westminster in 1834 and a public competition was held to choose an architect to design the new buildings. From 97 entries, Charles Barry's design was chosen as the winner and he enlisted the help of A W Pugin, the expert on authentic Gothic detailing. The result of their collaboration is a palatial building in the Tudor Perpendicular style, which perfectly fulfils its symbolic role as the building from which the nation is governed.

## INSIDE 'THE HOUSE'

The interior of 'The House' is a cramped warren containing 1,100 rooms, some 100 staircases and over 2 miles (3km) of corridor. The public areas are magnificently decorated in neo-Gothic and Arts and Crafts style. The actual debating chambers are so small that seating in the House of Commons can only accommodate 346 of the 650 elected Members of Parliament – the rest have to stand. This intimacy lends the House a club-like atmosphere which encourages the noisy barracking regarded by some as undignified and by others as an essential feature of parliamentary debate. The layout of the Commons, and of the second chamber, the House of Lords, reflects the fact that parliament formerly met in a chapel. The seating is ranged, like choir stalls, in parallel rows.

The House of Lords has been televised since 1985, and the House of Commons introduced the cameras, with trepidation, in November 1989. Some MPs reacted by employing 'personality stylists' to improve their TV images; and screen-conscious Members have been quick to introduce the 'doughnutting' technique during less popular debates, hurrying to fill the empty seats around whichever lonely MP is in shot, to give the impression of a full House.

Old fashioned street lamps on
Westminster Bridge cast a yellow
light as evening falls on the Houses
of Parliament

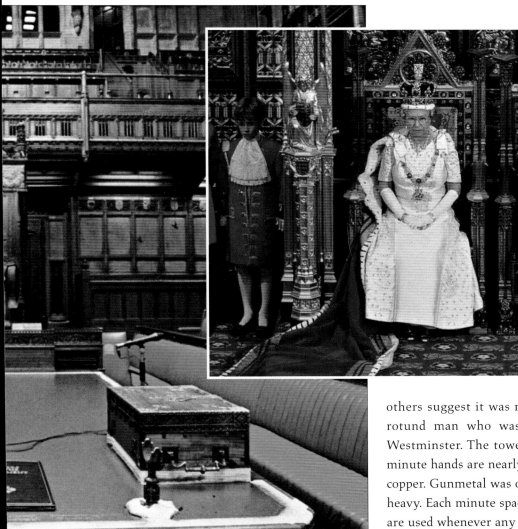

*LEFT At the State Opening of Parliament the Queen sets out the government's plans in her speech (actually written by the cabinet)*

## THE GUNPOWDER PLOT

◆

One of the most celebrated dates in British history is 5 November 1605, when Guido 'Guy' Fawkes and a number of other Roman Catholic conspirators attempted to blow up Parliament, along with James I and his ministers. Effigies of Guy Fawkes (and other unpopular figures) are burnt on bonfires at firework parties all over the country on this date, and the cellars of the House are still checked to this day by the Yeomen of the Guard before the ceremonial State Opening of Parliament.

others suggest it was named after Sir Benjamin Hall, the rotund man who was in charge of building works at Westminster. The tower has four massive clock faces; the minute hands are nearly 16ft (5m) long and made of hollow copper. Gunmetal was originally used, but proved to be too heavy. Each minute space is 11in (30cm) across. Old pennies are used whenever any slight adjustments are needed to the weight of the clock's pendulum – but only very rarely has the time been out by more than a fraction of a second.

## THE STATE OPENING OF PARLIAMENT

Following a general election and before each new session of Parliament in the autumn, there is a State Opening of Parliament, an event attended by much pomp and ceremony. In one of London's most colourful pageants, the Queen rides in the Irish State Coach from Buckingham Palace to the Palace of Whitehall, where she and other members of the royal family are greeted with a gun salute. The Queen, in full regalia, presides over the event from the House of Lords – no monarch has been admitted to the Commons since 1642, when Charles I forced his way in and tried to arrest five MPs, an event that sparked off the seven-year Civil War between Royalists and Parliamentarians.

## BIG BEN

Big Ben is the bell that tolls out the hours from the clock tower alongside the Houses of Parliament – a sound that is broadcast live at the beginning of television and radio news programmes. The first bell cracked in 1857, after it was cast, and had to be replaced with a new one, made in 1858. Nobody knows how the bell got its name. Some say it was named after 'Big Ben' Caunt, a heavyweight boxer of the day, while

# *Westminster Abbey*

**RIGHT** *Dean's Yard, to the south, offers one of the finest views of the graceful lines and the fine architectural detail of Westminster Abbey, with its splendid clock, inset*

**BELOW** *Rebuilt in the 13th century, Westminster Abbey was modelled on the great French cathedrals, such as Reims and Amiens*

**66**

HIS VAST AND SPLENDID GOTHIC BUILDING IS England's most important single church and national shrine. Every monarch since William the Conqueror has been crowned here, except Edward V (who was one of the murdered Princes in the Tower) and Edward VIII. Innumerable famous figures are also buried or commemorated here. First built by Edward the Confessor in the 11th century, the present church was begun 1245, and work continued into the early 1500s. The Henry VII Chapel was added early in the 16th century and the soaring west towers were added by Nicholas Hawksmoor in the 1730s to 1740s. Much restoration took place during the 18th and 19th centuries, prompting some protest. Since 1975, twenty years of cleaning and restoration has revealed the abbey in all its

splendour. To experience the full serenity of the building it is worth attending a service, not least to hear the choristers of Westminster School, accompanied by the abbey organ on which Henry Purcell (1659–95) once played.

## THE ORIGINS OF THE ABBEY

The abbey that gave its name to Westminster stood here in the 8th century, but the present building was begun by Edward the Confessor around 1050. He died a week after its consecration, on 6 January 1066, and was the first monarch to be buried here. His successor, Harold, was crowned here a week later, and William the Conqueror's coronation a year later confirmed the royal status of the church, which has seen the coronation of every subsequent English monarch.

Edward the Confessor was later canonised and Henry III embarked on large-scale rebuilding in 1245 to make a shrine fit for the veneration of the sainted king. Today's church, greatly influenced by the French Gothic cathedrals of Amiens and Reims, was the result. In 1503, the Lady Chapel at the east end was replaced by the Henry VII Chapel, the architectural high point of the church. The west front was not completed until 1745, when the two towers were built to Nicholas Hawksmoor's design.

## THE NAVE

Entering by the west door, visitors' eyes are drawn upwards to the majestic nave roof – a remarkable feature of the church is its great height (105ft/32m) in relation to its width. It is, in fact, the tallest Gothic nave in the country. The complex patterning of the vault then carries the eye eastwards; only by looking up can the enormous length of the building be properly appreciated, since at ground level the view is interrupted by the 19th-century screen that separates the nave from the choir and crossing.

The Tomb of the Unknown Warrior, one of the 1,000 monuments within the abbey, is straight ahead, and St George's Chapel, to the right, is now dedicated to the dead of the two World Wars. Just outside the chapel, on a pillar to the left, is a portrait of Richard II (1377–99), the oldest known true portrait of an English monarch.

Beyond the choir screen is the ceremonial heart of the church where services – and royal coronations – take place. There are good views to left and right of the huge and intricate rose windows of the transept. The sanctuary itself is railed off – the floor has a very rare cosmati-work pavement, a form of mosaic made of glass and precious stones, dated 1268, but this is usually covered by a carpet.

## POETS' CORNER

◆

Since the 16th century, the south transept has been the place where great poets and authors are honoured with memorials (though not all are buried here). Among the best monuments in Poets' Corner are the busts of Dryden, Jonson, Milton and Blake – the latter sculpted in bronze by Sir Jacob Epstein in 1957. There is also a fine statue of Shakespeare, paid for by public subscription and made in 1740. Two non-poets, though, have the finest monuments of all, both carved by Roubiliac – the composer Handel, on the west wall, holding pages from his oratorio *Messiah*, and the soldier-statesman John, Duke of Argyll and Greenwich, to the left of Handel, surrounded by figures symbolising Liberty, Eloquence and Wisdom.

69

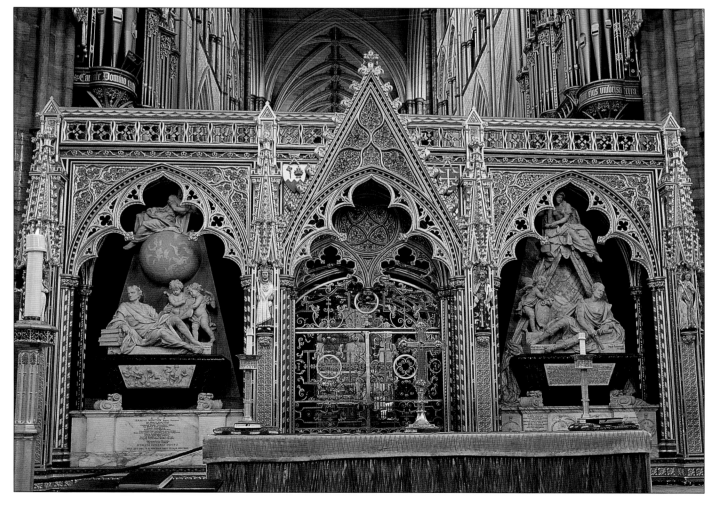

OPPOSITE *The abbey's interior, with its exquisite fan vaulting and soaring arches, is one of the finest achievements of English architecture*

LEFT *Separating the nave from the choir is this magnificent screen, richly coloured and intricately decorated, which dates from the 19th century*

## THE CHAPELS

Round the north side of the sanctuary is the north aisle of the Henry VII Chapel, with its white marble effigy of Elizabeth I, who shares a tomb with her half-sister, Mary I. The aisle leads to the main part of the Henry VII Chapel – the most exciting part of the abbey – with its exquisite fan-vaulted ceiling making an impressive setting for the royal tombs arranged around the altar and aisles. Among the finest of these is the tomb of Henry VII, in front of the altar, and of his mother, Lady Margaret Beaufort, near the south aisle altar. Mother and son both died in the same year (1509) Both tombs are the work of the Florentine sculptor, Pietro

Torrigiani, who, as a boy, was often involved in fights with Michelangelo. The tombs were the first examples of Renaissance carving to be seen in Britain; ironically, the king who built this chapel, the final flowering of Perpendicular Gothic architecture, is buried in a tomb whose Renaissance style was to eclipse the Gothic.

The chapel is used for installing Knights of the Bath, an order founded by Henry IV in 1399, and their banners hang above the flamboyant canopies of the wooden stalls. More down to earth are the stall misericords, carved with depictions of mermaids, monsters and a wife beating her husband.

A bridge leads from the Henry VII Chapel to the Confessor's Chapel, where the king who founded the abbey is buried, along with Henry III, who rebuilt it. Their tombs are plain by comparison with that of Queen Eleanor (died 1290), portrayed in an effigy of bronze. Here too is the wooden Coronation Chair made in 1300. It used to incorporate the ancient Scottish throne, the Stone of Scone, which dates back to at least the 9th century and was seized by Edward I in 1297, but in 1996 the stone was sent back to Scotland, to the delight of the Scots who had long campaigned for its return.

## CLOISTER, CHAPTER HOUSE AND MUSEUM

A door in the south choir aisle leads to the cloister, with its fine, flowing tracery and superb views of the flying buttresses that support the nave. The floor of the Chapter House, an octagonal building of 1253, is covered in its original tiles. It was here that parliament met between 1257 and 1547, before moving to the Palace of Westminster. One of the Abbey's highlights is the Norman undercroft, one of the few remaining parts of Edward the Confessor's original church, which houses the Abbey Treasures Museum. Here the macabre wax effigies of Queen Elizabeth I, Charles II and Admiral Nelson are displayed, made using death masks and the real clothes of the people they portray: Nelson's hat and eye-patch are those he wore in life. Some effigies were used to substitute the body for lyings-in-state; others were made in the 18th century to attract visitors to the Abbey.

The north transept contains monuments to many eminent statesmen, including Peel, Gladstone, Palmerston and Pitt the Elder, while the north choir aisle near the organ is dedicated to musicians, including Purcell, Elgar, Vaughan Williams and Britten. One of the best monuments here is to the relatively unknown Lady Elizabeth Nightingale. She died in 1731 (the monument erroneously says 1734) of a miscarriage, having been frightened by lightning. A dramatic monument by the great French sculptor Roubiliac (in the St Michael Chapel) depicts her lying in her husband's arms as Death aims his spear at her heart.

*OPPOSITE Highly detailed designs demonstrate the skill and dedication of the craftsmen who lovingly created this superb building over the centuries*

*RIGHT The splendid pulpit is a reminder that, although the abbey is a huge tourist attraction, it is still a place of worship with regular services*

# St James's Park

*S*ITUATED BETWEEN THE MALL, HORSE GUARD'S PARADE and Birdcage Walk, St James's Park is the most attractive of all London's green spaces, principally because of its lovely views. From the footbridge that crosses the lake at the heart of the park there are uninterrupted views westwards to the classical façade of Buckingham Palace, while to the east you see the rear of Sir George Gilbert Scott's glorious Government Offices, all turrets and onion domes, framed by the weeping willows whose branches cascade down to the fringes of the lake.

## BIRDS AND BUILDINGS

Several varieties of wildfowl add to the lake's attractions and many of the birds are quite tame, particularly with picnickers. Their number is swelled by migrant birds, and the park employs two full time ornithologists.

It is possible to take a stroll all the way round the perimeter of the lake, or to admire the views from the bridge and then head south to Birdcage Walk, the road that forms the southern park boundary. Its name comes from the aviaries that were here in the time of Charles II, continuing the tradition initiated by James I, who had a menagerie in the park. It included pelicans, crocodiles and even an elephant.

On the opposite side of the road, Cockpit Steps (a reminder that the birds were also used for sport) lead up to Queen Anne's Gate, a charming enclave of early 18th-century houses, several of them with very ornate wooden canopies over their front doors. There is a statue of Queen Anne in front of Number 15 and blue plaques abound, recording the famous people who were born here or who lived here in the past.

## THE LANDSCAPING OF THE PARK

The fields that were originally here were turned into a garden and deer park for St James's Palace by Henry VIII, and at that time it was reserved entirely for royal use. Charles I turned it into a formal garden, and it was through its leafy avenues that he walked to his death on the scaffold. After the

*Ornamental waterfowl have been a feature of the park since the time of the Stuart kings, and picnicking visitors ensure that they are well fed*

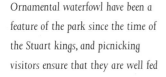

## CARLTON HOUSE TERRACE

◆

Parallel to the Mall and overlooking St James's Park, the elegant houses of this sweeping thoroughfare were built in the 1830s by John Nash on the site of the Prince Regent's Carlton House. Originally fashionable residences, the inhabitants included Mr Gladstone at Number 11 and Lord Curzon at Number 1; a statue of him by Sir Bertram Mackennal stands outside.

The buildings are now occupied by institutions such as The Royal Society at Number 6 and the Institute of Contemporary Arts at Number 12. Number 9 was the German Embassy from 1849 to 1939 and the gravestone of the embassy dog Giro, which died in 1934, is in the garden opposite. The street continues to Carlton Gardens, where Lord Palmerston and Lord Balfour both lived at Number 4, and where General de Gaulle had his headquarters from 1940. There is a statue of him opposite. Number 1, subsequently the Foreign Secretary's official residence, was once home to Prince Louis Napoleon (later Emperor Napoleon III). A statue of George VI, unveiled in 1955, looks towards the Mall at the top of the stairway.

*The gleaming white stone of Carlton House Terrace is a superb example of the work of John Nash, who shaped much of the London we see today*

Restoration, Charles II improved the park, employing the French landscape gardener, Le Nôtre, to turn it into a pleasure ground. The king, who liked to walk his spaniels here, subsequently opened the park to the public. Le Nôtre's work was swept away under George IV, who commissioned John Nash to give the park a more naturalistic look. Nash created the fine meandering lake, with its central bridge, that still lends so much charm to the park today.

LEFT *Delightful features, such as this charming bridge and cascade, all contribute to the popularity of London's most attractive park*

# Trafalgar Square

The four famous lions which guard the foot of Nelson's Column were cast in bronze from a single original sculpture by Edwin Landseer

CENTRE Constantly surrounded by the roar of London traffic, Trafalgar Square gives the accurate feeling of being at the very hub of the capital

A T THE NORTH END OF WHITEHALL, TRAFALGAR SQUARE is probably second only to Piccadilly Circus as a well-known London location and meeting point. On a site where hawks lived in the medieval royal mews, later royal stables, the square is now populated by disorderly pigeons. The principal creator of today's square was John Nash and it was laid out during the 1830s to 1840s.

The square is surrounded by fine buildings, including the National Gallery, the church of St Martin-in-the-Fields, 1930s South Africa House, Admiralty Arch and the 1820s classical Canada House. In the centre is the lofty Nelson's Column, constructed in the 1840s and topped by a giant statue of Lord Nelson, with guardian lions below by Landseer. The famous fountains were remodelled 1939 by Lutyens, and the site features a number of statues, including an equestrian statue of Charles I looking down Whitehall; a wreath is laid here on anniversary of his execution. Others include Sir Henry Havelock, with a police box beneath; Sir Charles Napier; an equestrian statue of George IV with no stirrups by Chantrey, and busts of Admirals Cunningham, Jellicoe and Beatty against the north wall.

## LONDON'S RALLYING POINT

Trafalgar Square has a long tradition as a place where crowds gather – and not just the everyday crush of tourists and pigeon-feeders. This is the place to be for carol singing on Christmas eve or to see in the New Year, and is a traditional place for political meetings and demonstrations. Among the most famous of these were the annual Aldermaston Marches of the 1950s and 60s, when supporters of the Campaign for Nuclear Disarmament trudged from the Atomic Weapons Establishment in Aldermaston, Berkshire to Trafalgar Square for a huge Easter rally.

## ST MARTIN'S IN THE FIELD

This lovely church is by far the best building in Trafalgar Square. Built by James Gibbs between 1721 and 1726, the church resembles a classical temple, except for the fine spire

Standing over 56m high, Nelson's Column, commemorating the great naval hero, is one of London's most famous landmarks

which is just a fraction taller than Nelson's Column. If the arrangement of portico and steeple seems familiar, it is because this architectural masterpiece inspired many a church in early colonial America. Inside, either side of the chancel, are boxes for members of the royal family (on the left) and the staff of the Admiralty, whose office is near by in Whitehall. This was the original home of the Academy of St Martin-in-the-Fields, the well-known orchestra, and the free lunchtime concerts here, given by a variety of musical

## ADMIRALTY ARCH

◆

Built in 1910 as a memorial to Queen Victoria and to lead the processional way to Buckingham Palace, this magnificent sweeping arch separates the chaotic traffic of Trafalgar Square from the relative calm of the Mall. The rooms above the arch are government offices, part of the old Admiralty Building, and plans to turn them into luxury apartments have also been proposed. To the left is the grim and windowless Citadel, built as a bomb shelter for Admiralty staff in 1940.

*TOP On the anniversary of the Battle of Trafalgar – October 1805 – a naval parade passes through Admiralty Arch before a service in the square*

groups, are very popular. The church has long been known as a refuge for the homeless; nowadays it also houses a bookshop, brass rubbing centre, art gallery and café (in the crypt), while a craft market is located at the rear.

St Martin-in-the-Fields is often referred to as the 'church of the homeless'. This is because Dick Sheppard, vicar from 1914 to 1927, opened a shelter in the crypt just after World War I to help unemployed and destitute ex-soldiers. Today the work is continued with soup kitchens and with general assistance for the homeless in the parish rooms' basement. Many famous people are associated with the church: George I was the first churchwarden here, and his coat of arms appears on the pediment and above the chancel arch; Charles II was christened in an earlier church on this site in 1630 and his mistress, Nell Gwyn, was buried in the churchyard, as was Thomas Chippendale. The original burial ground was, however, cleared in 1829 to make room for Duncannon Street to the south.

# The Nation's Galleries

Along the north side of Trafalgar Square are two of the world's foremost art galleries: the National Gallery and the National Portrait Gallery, housing the national collection of western paintings from the 13th century to modern times.

## The National Gallery

The building offers a superb view across the square from its entrance terrace. Two bronze statues stand on the lawns on either side of the entrance: one of James II dressed as a Roman, by Grinling Gibbons (1686), and one of George Washington, presented by the American people in 1921.

The National was founded in 1824 to house a national art collection to compete with the European galleries. By coincidence the Pall Mall house of John Julius Angerstein was for sale at the time, along with his collection of 38 paintings, including works by Rembrandt and Van Dyck. These were bought for £57,000 and Angerstein's house served as the first gallery until the completion of the present building in 1838. Meanwhile, the collection grew through gifts and bequests,

but many of the most famous works were acquired by shrewd directors scouring Europe for masterpieces that could be bought cheaply – those by artists temporarily 'out of fashion'. Lack of space dictated a policy of quality rather than quantity, resulting in one of the world's richest collections.

## The Main Gallery

A bridge leads from the Sainsbury Wing to the main gallery, which includes well-loved paintings such as Constable's *The Haywain* and Seurat's *Une Baignade, Asnières*. The West Wing features the 16th-century works of art, including Michelangelo's *Entombment*, the North Wing is devoted to 17th-century artists such as Van Dyck, Rubens, Rembrandt, Velázquez and painters of the Dutch school, and the East Wing moves on with works by Chardin, Gainsborough, Monet, Matisse, Seurat and Picasso.

The floor mosaics of the main staircase and vestibules were designed by Russian-born Boris Anrep between 1928 and 1952. Those in the west vestibule illustrate the Labours of Life, while those in the north include portrals of Winston Churchill and T S Eliot exemplifying Defiance and Leisure, in

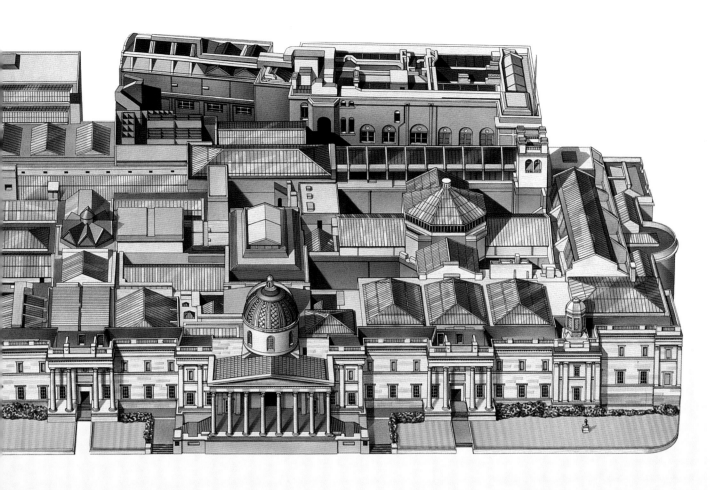

77

## THE SAINSBURY WING

◆

The controversial new Sainsbury Wing annexe is entered at the extreme left of the main entrance. Earlier plans for the site, incorporating an office block, were abandoned after Prince Charles described the proposed building as 'a carbuncle on the well-loved face of Trafalgar Square'. As a result, the Sainsbury family, owners of the supermarket chain, donated the funds for today's building, designed by Robert Venturi — another source of controversy, since an American architect was chosen in preference to a British one.

Since the annexe houses Renaissance works, the architect incorporated motifs inspired by 16th-century Italian palazzi. Brilliantly coloured paintings are dramatically framed by doorway arches carved in grey pietra serena, the stone that lends such grace to many of the best Italian Renaissance buildings. Thus the annexe makes a fitting and complementary setting for the varied works of Jan van Eyck, Botticelli, Uccello and for Leonardo da Vinci's entrancing cartoon, the *Virgin and Child*.

the *Modern Virtues* series. Best of all, the *Awakening of the Muses* on the mezzanine includes portraits of the most beautiful women of the 1930s: Greta Garbo as Melpemone (Muse of Tragedy), Virginia Woolf as Clio (Muse of History) and Diana Mitford as Polyhymnia (Muse of Song).

## THE NATIONAL PORTRAIT GALLERY

Tucked away behind the National Gallery, the National Portrait Gallery houses a fascinating collection of some 7,000 paintings, drawings, sculptures and photographs depicting famous figures from every facet of British history and life. The collection is based on the eminence of the subject, regardless of the merits of the artist, but even so, many important artists are represented, from Hans Holbein to David Hockney, and the collection provides an intriguing overview of the development of portraiture.

The works are displayed chronologically, with the earliest on the top floor. Among the medieval portraits are the 14th-century poet Geoffrey Chaucer and his patron, Richard II, portrayed as a sensitive and beautiful young man (this is a copy of the original portrait in Westminster Abbey). Two towering monarchs dominate the Tudor Rooms: Holbein's Henry VIII is surrounded by several wives and advisers who fell from grace; Elizabeth I is accompanied by favourites such as the Earls of Leicester and Essex.

Although monarchs, politicians and soldiers dominate the early part of the collection, later rooms have a fair share of writers, artists and scientists, including Shakespeare, Donne, Milton, Pepys, Sir Christopher Wren and Sir Isaac Newton. Among the most popular pictures are the romantic portrait of the young Lord Byron, the only known portrait of Jane Austen (by her sister Cassandra) and a tender portrait of the Brontë sisters by their brother Branwell.

The late Victorian and 20th-century displays are among the most striking, especially since they show artists seeking new ways to get beneath the skin of their subject and make a statement about their essential characters. Many are self-portraits or depictions of one artist by another. Needless to say, the recent royal portraits of the young Diana, Princess of Wales, of Prince Charles in polo gear (both painted by Bryan Organ) and of Queen Elizabeth II (by Pietro Annigoni) attract a great deal of discussion and interest.

# The West End

London's Chinatown is coloured by its bright shop fronts and perfumed by the kitchens of its many authentic regional restaurants

THE HEART OF LONDON IS A VIBRANT AREA OF PUBS AND clubs, cinemas and theatres, cosmopolitan cafés and restaurants and bustling squares. It is the site of Soho, Covent Garden and of Leicester Square, a mecca for those out for entertainment in the city.

## SOHO AND CHINATOWN

A mere two decades ago, Soho was a byword for sex clubs and sleaze, and Covent Garden was the run-down haunt of vegetable and flower traders. When the wholesale market moved to modern premises in 1974, the whole future of Covent Garden looked uncertain. Eventually, the market halls were converted into small shops and stalls, and this became a largely traffic-free area where buskers entertain and visitors can relax in pavement cafés. Soho blossomed, too, as a determined effort was made to clean up the area.

Pretty Soho Square is where office workers from the film, advertising and design companies of nearby Dean Street and Wardour Street come to eat lunchtime sandwiches, while the executives enjoy expense-account lunches in the restaurants of Greek Street, which leads southwards out of the square. Old Compton Street is another gourmets' haven, while Berwick Street market is the best in London for fresh fruit and vegetables.

At the heart of London's large Chinatown quarter is Gerrard Street, now a colourful pedestrian precinct; top-quality Chinese restaurants line Wardour Street, which leads to the cinemas of Leicester Square, most famous of which is

Berwick Street market brings together the highest-quality produce and an atmosphere of good-humoured banter in the heart of Soho

the Odeon, scene of many star-studded London premieres. The mechanical clock on the façade of the Swiss Centre in the square is a popular attraction when it performs on the hour.

## LONG ACRE AND THE ROYAL OPERA HOUSE

To the north-east is Long Acre, Covent Garden's main thoroughfare, leading to the covered market and to Bow Street, from where the Bow Street Runners, a prototype police force, operated in the early 19th-century. Opposite Bow Street Magistrate's Court is the Royal Opera House, home to both the Royal Opera and the Royal Ballet. Fronted by E M Barry's Corinthian façade and John Flaxman's Grecian frieze, purists pay huge sums to come here to see opera performed 'as it should be'. However, prestigious productions are mounted in conditions that have improved little since 1858, when the stage and dressing rooms were built.

*The whole of Soho has a cosmopolitan feel to it, but in pedestrianised Gerrard Street the capital's Chinese quarter is well and truly to the fore*

WHOLE FRUIT & FLAVOURED INFUSIONS

*The whole spectrum of places to eat and drink can be found in the West End, from acclaimed gourmet restaurants to the traditional teashop*

*RIGHT Covent Garden's covered mall, teeming with a huge variety of quality shops and busy places to eat, is justifiably popular at any time*

*BELOW The Neal's Yard area of town is a pleasure to stroll around, with its maze of innumerable specialist shops, studios and art galleries*

## SHOPS AND RESTAURANTS

To the north of Long Acre is a maze of little streets, some lined with warehouses once used to store fruit and vegetables, but now converted to dance studios, art galleries and specialist shops, the pick of which are in Neal Street. Some of the best food shops are found in the old warehouses surrounding Neal's Yard, which is a gourmet's paradise. One thing to look out for, in more ways than one, is the sculpture on the opposite side of the yard, which consists of several wooden figures in a queue. This is animated by putting a coin in a slot, the surprise comes when the man at the end of the queue spits a powerful jet of water at unwary onlookers.

## COVENT GARDEN

This is the spirited heart of central London, a mini-community within the city, but with important differences. One is the freedom to roam largely free of traffic. Another is the fact that the shops are small, personal and sell a wide range of interesting products, from buttons and bows to books and works of art. The focal point is the Central Market, an elegant building designed by Charles Fowler and completed in the 1830s, although the iron and glass roof over the central arcade was added in the 1870s. The wholesale fruit and vegetable market that operated here was relocated in 1974, after which the site was converted to provide space for the scores of small specialist shops and cafés that now line the arcade, itself filled with market stalls selling antiques, crafts, toys, jewellery and clothing.

The Punch and Judy pub, on the south-western corner of the market, opened in 1980, but its name is a reminder that the first Punch and Judy puppet show was performed in the square below on 9 May 1662 – Samuel Pepys was among those who came to watch the antics of Pietro Gimonde's marionettes. Mr Punch's birthday is still celebrated on the

second Sunday in May, as part of the Covent Garden May Fayre. Entertainment takes place here all week from 10am to dusk: the space in front of St Paul's Church is used by street performers – clowns, fire-eaters, musicians, acrobats – and the day's programme is posted on the church railings which frame the entrance to the Victorian public lavatories built below the square, an attraction in their own right.

## THE LONDON TRANSPORT MUSEUM

Housed in the old Covent Garden Flower Market, this is a far more enthralling museum than its name suggests. Children can climb aboard the buses and trams or pretend to drive underground trains, while adults contemplate the sheer immensity and complexity of London's transport system.

The red double-decker bus has long been an internationally recognised symbol of the city, and the development of London's bus system is illustrated by replicas of early horse-drawn transport. These include Mr Shillibeer's omnibus of 1829, which brought a whole new era of mobility to Londoners. Surprisingly, the idea was not invented in Britain – Shillibeer's inspiration came from the French town of Nantes, where a Monsieur Omnès had been operating passenger vehicles under his company's Latin slogan (also a pun on his own name) of *Omnes Omnibus* ('all for everyone'). Also on display is one of the first motorised buses, the Type B, known as 'Old Bill', which came into operation as early as 1897. The progression from horse-drawn transport was not immediate, however, but was eventually hastened by the onset of World War I, when the demand for horses on the battlefields led to their disappearance from London's streets.

Another vintage vehicle on display is the railway locomotive built in 1866 to operate on the Metropolitan Line, fitted with a device which enabled it to consume its own

## THEATRE MUSEUM

◆

This splendid museum really works hard to involve visitors (especially children) in the magic of the theatre, with a programme of activities and special exhibitions covering everything from make-up demonstrations to dressing up in theatrical costumes. Permanent displays trace the history of the stage since the 16th century using models, props and costumes, bringing the subject right up to date with a look at the glamorous world of rock music — Mick Jagger's jumpsuit is a popular exhibit.

The collection is arranged chronologically and is so varied that, like the theatre itself, the scene constantly shifts to present new surprises. Here visitors come face to face with Hamlet, the great actors who have starred in the role, their costumes and historical set designs; and for a little light relief, there are displays about the pantomime dame or the perennially popular farce *Charley's Aunt*, written in 1892 and still regularly performed all over the country. You can see the dressing table where the great 18th-century actress, Sarah Siddons, used to apply her make-up before entrancing audiences in the role of Lady Macbeth, or admire Noel Coward's crimson monogrammed dressing gown and slippers. Other striking exhibits include the costumes worn by dancers in the innovative ballets choreographed by Diaghilev and the wheelbarrow used by the famous acrobat Blondin in his daring highwire acts.

The London Palladium, which opened on Boxing Day 1910, has reigned supreme as the foremost venue for top-name variety shows and pantomime

smoke. The first underground service, which opened in 1904, was operated by electric trains and opened up a whole new era. Londoners began to move to new garden cities and suburban estates on the city's fringes, and thus the age of the commuter was born. To promote their services, London Transport hired some of the best graphic artists of the day to design posters, many of which are on display in the museum.

## THEATRELAND

Some 40 theatres are packed into the area of London known as Theatreland, consisting of Haymarket, St Martin's Lane, Shaftesbury Avenue and Charing Cross Road. This area comes to life after dark, as the audiences arrive to enjoy the illuminated façades, glittering interiors and intimate atmospheres of its Victorian and Edwardian theatres.

One of the oldest West-End theatres is the Theatre Royal, Drury Lane, founded in 1663, when London's appetite for theatre was all the more keen after 20 years of Oliver Cromwell's puritanical rule, during which play-going was forbidden. It was here that Charles II first set eyes on Nell Gwyn, who was to become his mistress; and it was here that, during the 1740s, David Garrick revived Shakespeare's plays,

scarcely performed since the bard's death. The foyer and staircases are worth seeing for the impressive collection of statues and paintings of famous actors and managers.

The London Palladium, in Argyll Street, is the work of the prolific theatre designer, Frank ('Matchless') Matcham. He built 80 theatres during his 40-year career, and was renowned for his lavish, flamboyant style. The Palladium interior is still a frothy confection of gold, white and scarlet, but now lacks the box-to-box telephones that enabled amorous members of the audience to arrange post-theatre assignations. The theatre is famous for its pantomimes and for hosting the annual Royal Command Performance.

Previous command performances took place at the Theatre Royal, Haymarket, and such was the crowd awaiting the first, in 1794, that 15 people were crushed to death. The present theatre, built by Nash in 1820, specialises in 'quality' plays and has a resident ghost — that of Queen Victoria's favourite actor-manager, Mr Buckstone. Right opposite is Her Majesty's Theatre, originally built in 1704 by playwright and architect Sir John Vanbrugh, and rebuilt in 1897 in French Renaissance style. Many renowned operas received their first English performances here, including Wagner's *Ring*.

OPPOSITE *Actor-guides, simulators and hands-on exhibits bring to life the most fascinating aspects of the world's largest urban public transport system*

# Banqueting House

O NE OF BRITAIN'S MOST IMPORTANT ARCHITECTURAL monuments, the Banqueting House was built between 1619 and 1622 by Inigo Jones, who had trained in Livorno in Tuscany and absorbed the influence of Palladio. He introduced the purity of classical design to London, initially with the Queen's House at Greenwich (now part of the National Maritime Museum complex), and later with this sophisticated and seminal building.

### THE EXTERIOR

The Banqueting House is now so hemmed in by other classical buildings that it is difficult to imagine how exotic

*By means of this mirror, visitors can appreciate the magnificent ceiling of the Banqueting House, the only surviving part of Whitehall Palace*

and different it would once have appeared, crisply faced in white Portland stone and surrounded by the ramshackle brick and timber buildings that were typical of Tudor London.

The House occupies part of the site of the former Whitehall Palace, acquired – or rather seized – by Henry VIII from Cardinal Wolsey and used for courtly entertainment. When fire destroyed part of the palace, James I employed Inigo Jones to rebuild it on a massive scale – it was to be modelled on the Tuileries Palace in Paris – but only the Banqueting House was ever completed.

## PAINTED CEILINGS

While the exterior is relatively restrained, except for the festive frieze of garlands running beneath the parapet, the colourful ceiling paintings inside provide a powerful contrast. They were commissioned by Charles I and designed by Peter Paul Rubens, who was knighted for this work. Painted in Antwerp, and installed in 1635, the nine pictures are intended to emphasise the divine authority of the monarch, a contentious political issue at the time. James I, Charles' father, is shown being received into heaven while other scenes depict the claimed benefits of his rule – peace, prosperity and the Union of England and Scotland.

Rubens' ceiling paintings are quite ironic in the light of subsequent events, for Charles I went to his execution from this room on 30 January 1649, having fought and lost the seven-year Civil War. A scaffold was erected outside the Banqueting House and it was from here, through a window, that Charles I stepped out on to the scaffold to meet his death. A bust of Charles I over the staircase entrance marks the probable site of that window

*This sumptuously decorated ceiling, such a delight to visitors today, was one of the last things that Charles I saw before his execution in 1649*

# Somerset House

Somerset House still houses an odd mix of government departments. One of them is the Inland Revenue, responsible for collecting income tax, as well as death duties, stamp tax and land duty fees. Here too is the Principal Probate Registry, which holds copies of every will registered since 1858. For a fee the public is entitled to see any they choose. Immediately to the east of is King's College, founded in 1828 by the Duke of Wellington, then Prime Minister, and the Archbishop of Canterbury. It was set up as a reaction to the founding of University College in 1826, called 'the godless institution' because divinity was not on the syllabus; in contrast, King's put religion at the core of its teaching.

## Courtauld Institute Galleries

Some of the world's most famous Impressionist paintings are to be seen in the treasure-filled Courtauld Institute Galleries, part of London University. The core of this collection was assembled by the textile magnate Samuel Courtauld (1876–1947), who gave the pictures to the Institute that bears his name in 1931, with the aim of providing students of art history with outstanding works that they could study in close detail. His gift was expanded when the art critic, Roger Fry, and other major patrons also donated their private collections. In 1990 the whole collection was moved to the rooms of the Strand Block at Somerset House, where they are hung to advantage beneath the ornate plaster ceilings. The galleries are specially notable for the magnificent Courtauld collection of French Impressionists and Post-Impressionists (Cézanne, Degas, Monet, Seurat and so on).

## A Monumental Setting

The entrance to Somerset House is through a triple-arched gateway fronting the Strand. Façade sculptures symbolising oceans and rivers, the Cardinal Virtues and the Genius of Britain reinforce the building's monumental stature. Within is a courtyard with more façade sculptures – of the Arms of Britain, the tritons and the Continents, and George III with the River Thames at his feet. The key to all this grandiloquence is the fact that Somerset House was built from 1776 to house important offices of state, among them the Navy Office, the Exchequer and the Audit Office, the forerunners of today's government ministries. The Strand Block, home of the Courtauld Galleries, originally housed the Royal Academy, the Royal Society and the Society of Antiquaries, and their classically inspired fittings have remained, including the elegant staircase and the ceiling decorations, which are only awaiting the necessary funds to be restored to their original colouring.

## The Galleries

The ceiling of the first gallery has the initials RA (for Royal Academy) worked into it, along with pairs of paintbrushes in the corner. Among the 15th- and 16th-century paintings here

**LEFT AND BELOW** *Somerset House,*
*built in 1776, accommodates the*
*Courtauld Institute Galleries and is*
*also home to some public bodies*

are Renaissance masterpieces such as Botticelli's *Holy Trinity with Saint John and Mary Magdalen* (1490–4). Parmigianino's *Virgin and Child* (1524–7) is an example of the High Renaissance or Mannerist style, characterised by brilliant colouring and contorted figures. Gallery 2 has the finest ceiling, and houses several masterpieces such as Rubens' *Descent from the Cross* (1611) – a *modello*, or trial piece, for his most famous 'Antwerp Descent', the great altarpiece in Antwerp Cathedral.

Gallery 3 has the initials of the Society of Antiquaries worked into the ceiling, and features more paintings by Rubens. Gallery 4 is devoted to 18th-century Italian art, and Gallery 5, the Royal Society Meeting Room, is where plaster portraits of the Society's founder, Charles II, and of George III look down on the gorgeously coloured works of Manet, Degas, Renoir and Pissarro. Manet's *Bar at the Folies-Bergère*

(1882) is the most eye-catching, and his *Déjeuner sur l'Herbe* (1863) is a smaller version of the painting in the Musée d'Orsay in Paris. Here, too, is Van Gogh's *Self-portrait with Bandaged Ear,* a reminder of the quarrel that the artist had with Gauguin (Van Gogh threatened his friend with a knife, then cut off part of his own ear in remorse). The next gallery and rooms on the floors above cover Post-Impressionist works and also works by 20th-century British artists, as well as changing exhibitions. The largest of these rooms, Gallery 8, the Great Room, was used for Royal Academy summer exhibitions until 1836. The 'RA Line' runs round the room, a moulding set 6 ½ft (2m) or so above the floor. Favoured works to which the RA Hanging Committee wanted to give prominence were hung below the line; less favoured works were 'skied' above it; the term refers to the fact that the ceiling was originally painted to resemble the sky.

# Royal Academy of Arts

*This statue of Raphaël is just one of several eminent figures represented by carvings on the imposing façade of the Royal Academy*

HE PRESTIGIOUS ROYAL ACADEMY OF ARTS, WHOSE members include many well-known British artists and architects, was founded in 1768 under the patronage of George III, with Sir Joshua Reynolds as its first president. The building is used for major art exhibitions, which change regularly but are always deservedly popular, since they feature masterpieces of art on loan from museums and collections around the world.

## BURLINGTON HOUSE

Home of the Royal Academy, Burlington House is Piccadilly's most imposing structure, built as a Palladian-style *palazzo* (mansion) for the Earl of Burlington around 1720. It is set back from the street and the courtyard in front has a statue of Sir Joshua Reynolds, who, as first President of the Academy, was charged with raising the prestige of the arts and of providing tuition to promising painters (Constable and Turner were among the first students). The statues which adorn the façade were carved by various hands and represent Raphaël, Titian, Wren and Leonardo da Vinci, among many other eminent figures.

The two wings on either side house the offices, libraries and meeting rooms of other learned bodies, such as the Society of Antiquaries. The main entrance is straight ahead and the entrance hall, with its grand ceremonial staircase, features ceiling paintings by former Academicians – notably Benjamin West's *The Graces and The Four Elements*.

## THE EXHIBITION ROOMS

The main exhibition rooms are on the first floor, and many of them have splendid doorcases, ceiling decorations and fireplaces. The top floor of the building houses the Sackler Galleries, reached by a glass lift. It has recently been remodelled by Sir Norman Foster, himself an Academician, and is used for smaller exhibitions, including shows by living artists. Here is Michelangelo's *Madonna and Child with the infant St John*, a circular relief carved in marble in 1504–5 and considered to be one of his most beautiful works.

*OPPOSITE Located behind a courtyard, imposing Burlington House has been remodelled extensively since construction began in about 1664*

*RIGHT The vast ceremonial staircase leading from the entrance hall of Burlington House features ceiling paintings by former Academicians*

One of the high points of the London Season is the Royal Academy Summer Exhibition, and tickets to the fashionable and exclusive private preview are eagerly sought. The exhibition, which lasts from June until mid-August, displays the paintings, sculpture and architectural drawings of living artists, and much of the work is for sale. Of the 10,000 or so works submitted, the Academicians select just over 1,000 for public display. Despite past criticism for conservatism, the choice today tends to be more adventurous.

89

# Mayfair and Piccadilly

THIS AREA OF LONDON INCLUDES SOME OF THE MOST famous thorougfares and shopping streets, stretching from the bustling universal meeting place at Piccadilly Circus, along the sweeping expanse of Regent Street and up to Bond Street and Oxford Street. Mayfair also contains some of London's most elegant houses, set around leafy squares, affordable only by governments (as embassies), large companies and multi-millionaires, and some of the most opulent and famous hotels in the world.

## PICCADILLY

This long street between Piccadilly Circus and Hyde Park Corner was still just a rural lane around 1650. Piccadilly takes its name from a mansion built here in 1612 for one Robert Baker, who had made his fortune selling 'picadils', a type of stiff collar fashionable with the 17th-century court. His house (and the area surrounding it) thus became known as Piccadilly. Today, Piccadilly is an intriguing mix of gaudy neon, gentlemen's clubs and splendid old shops. Piccadilly Circus, with its garish giant neon signs, is probably the best-known location in all London. Laid out in around 1820 by John Nash, the site is famed for the statue of Eros, a monument to the famous philanthropist Lord Shaftesbury, designed by Sir Alfred Gilbert in 1893. The London Pavilion

*OPPOSITE The neon lights of Piccadilly Circus are as familiar a landmark as Eros and add colour to this busy junction and meeting point*

*RIGHT The statue known as Eros was erected in 1892 as a memorial to Lord Shaftesbury and represents the Angel of Christian Charity*

*Many exclusive shops are to be found in Burlington Arcade and along Regent Street, Bond Street, Oxford Street and Piccadilly*

and the Trocadero are brash, noisy entertainment, restaurant and shopping complexes, always brimming with young people. The centre includes the Rock Circus pop music show, the Guinness World of Records exhibition of superlatives and Segaworld, the ultimate in amusement arcades.

On the south side the Criterion Restaurant has been restored to High Victorian splendour and, going west, the grandly pillared front of Le Meridien Piccadilly (the former Piccadilly Hotel) is by Richard Norman Shaw. Then come St James's Church, with its interesting weekly market and brass rubbings, Fortnum and Mason – purveyors of groceries to the rich and famous – the Royal Academy and Burlington Arcade. Located on Piccadilly next to the Royal Academy, the arcade is London's best-known shopping arcade, enclosing several exclusive boutiques. It was built in 1819 and given its ornate front by Beresford Pite in 1931. The arcade has uniformed beadles, and traditional rules forbid singing, running and carrying opened umbrellas.

Further along Piccadilly the Ritz Hotel is followed by Green Park, a pleasantly simple Royal park of plain grass and trees between Piccadilly and Constitution Hill. It was first enclosed in the 1660s by Charles II and Constitution Hill is said to owe its name to his habit of taking his daily walk or 'constitutional' there.

## REGENT STREET

Named after the Prince Regent, later George IV, the street was laid out by John Nash between 1813 and 1816 to form a grand boulevard linking Regent's Park with the royal palaces and aristocratic mansions of Carlton House and Pall Mall. Though most of the original buildings have been replaced, Regent Street retains its grandeur, especially at the Piccadilly Circus end, where it bends dramatically to the left, obscuring the buildings that lie beyond but promising much. Running parallel behind Regent Street is Carnaby Street, once a byword for trendiness and now regaining a little of its former glory after years in decline.

Many of its best buildings (and the best shops) are on the eastern side of Regent Street and include the Café Royal, once the haunt of Aubrey Beardsley and Oscar Wilde, and Garrard & Co, jewellers to the seriously wealthy, including the royal family. Other famous names include the well respected clothes shops Aquascutum and Burberry's, the wondrous Hamley's toy shop, Laura Ashley, Dickins & Jones and, of course, Liberty's.

## BOND STREET

◆

New Bond Street and Old Bond Street together run from Oxford Street south to Piccadilly. This area is synonymous with style and there is a concentration of art dealers and smart shops, including Asprey's, the luxury jewellers founded by William Asprey in the 1780s. This is also the site of Sotheby's auction house, founded in 1744.

*Liberty's is renowned for its wide range of fine goods and fabrics, with items from around the world displayed bazaar-style in this elegant building*

## LIBERTY'S

Occupying numbers 210–20 Regent Street is a department store unlike any other in London: an Aladdin's Cave housed in a building that is a gem of Arts and Crafts design, packed with goods from around the world, from African tribal jewellery to brightly patterned fabrics, all arranged to recreate the atmosphere of a bazaar. By contrast, the top floor resembles an informal museum: on one side is Arts and Crafts furniture, known for the beautiful patina of its wood and its straightforward, clean design, and on the other, glass cases line the walls, filled with antique silver and pewter pieces specially commissioned from artists such as Archibald Knox; his flowing, Celtic-inspired designs were so popular that 'Liberty style' became synonymous with art nouveau. The Liberty print is still the main attraction – immediately recognisable and carrying a stylish image, and the central stairwell looks down on oriental carpets and Liberty's own range of fabrics. In the packed basement are the Japanese ceramics, textiles and prints that were Arthur Lasenby Liberty's trade mark when he opened the store in 1875.

The store's Tudor-style wing dates from 1924 and is built of timbers salvaged from HMS *Impregnable* and HMS *Hindustan*. A bridge across Kingly Street, linking the shop's two parts, features a clock where St George and the Dragon do battle every hour. Above the Great Marlborough Street entrance is a gilded caravel, the sailing ship that once carried cargoes of silks, porcelain and spices; over the Regent Street entrance a frieze shows Britannia receiving goods from the nations of the world.

## OXFORD STREET

Originally a Roman road between London and the west, this was named after the Earl of Oxford, whose daughter married one of the Dukes of Portland. The street was not built up until the 18th century, and became an important shopping thoroughfare in the 19th century. Immensely crowded with tourists, noisy and often described as an approximation of hell on earth, its shops range from gimcrack tourist traps to stately department stores, including Debenhams, D H Evans, John Lewis, Marks and Spencer and Selfridges.

The queen of the Oxford Street stores, Selfridges department store was founded by the American entrepreneur Harry Gordon Selfridge and opened in 1909. This giant building of genuine grandeur, with tall Ionic columns and a huge art deco clock, is famed for its huge perfume department and excellent food hall.

## STATELY SQUARES

The area covering Mayfair and Piccadilly takes in some of London's most exclusive and stylish squares, some of whose

buildings are used for the major embassies. Grosvenor Square, one of London's largest, was laid out by the Grosvenor family in the 1720s, and much has changed since. The fortress-like American Embassy occupies the west side, adorned with a huge eagle. The embassy grounds feature several statues and memorials, including Presidents Franklin D Roosevelt and Eisenhower, and a Memorial to the Royal Air Force American Eagle Squadron. In April 1994 a stone inscribed 'The Nation Gives Thanks' was unveiled to dedicate Grosvenor Square Gardens as a permanent D-Day garden of remembrance.

*ABOVE The elegant Orangerie, a private dining room at Claridges, one of London's premier hotels, is a superb setting for a meal*

*LEFT Oxford Street is one of the busiest streets in London, with visitors constantly risking life and limb between endless buses and taxis*

## LIVING IT UP

This area also features some of the finest, most luxurious hotels in the world, places to be pampered in sumptuous surroundings by staff who maintain traditional standards of professionalism. Overlooking Hyde Park, the splendid Berkeley Hotel is both modern, in the up-to-date facilities it provides, and stylishly traditional in its discreet and restful atmosphere. Its Asian restaurant is extremely fashionable, complementing the traditional Anglo-French cuisine of the main restaurant.

Claridges has been welcoming visiting royalty, heads of state and some of the world's most illustrious families for about 100 years and has kept many of its original features, including the wonderful black and white marble front hall foyer. The atmosphere is regal and the service is very formal.

Built in the 1930s and splendidly refurbished in the early 1990s, The Dorchester Hotel is one of the most famous of London's hotels, its very name synonymous with luxury and privilege. Its glittering interiors include three superb restaurants, elegant lounges and some of the most expensive suites in the capital.

Some of the longer-established of London's luxury hotels can tend to be a little snobbish, but the Four Seasons is a modern hotel with a modern attitude, combining first-class, professional service with a more friendly approach.

Internationally recognised for its luxury and exceptionally fine cuisine, the Grosvenor House Hotel is housed in the 1920s replacement for the town mansion of the Dukes of Westminster with a west front by Lutyens. Accommodation here includes a wing of fully serviced apartments.

Since the Hilton bought up, and subsequently gave its name to, a couple of chains of budget hotels, the name has lost some of its former magic. But this is the original Hilton, and as such is as glamorous as ever. The 28th floor of this 1960s' tower houses the Windows Restaurant, with wonderful views over Hyde Park.

César Ritz established this famous eponymous hotel in 1906 and introduced a new word into the language – Ritzy sums up all the glamour and glitter that he offered his guests, and even though the hotel has had mixed fortunes in recent years, the image remains.

95

### A TASTE OF THE HIGH LIFE

◆

Many whose budgets do not run to even a single night of luxury in one of London's top hotels have discovered the perfect way of enjoying the atmosphere and feeling, at least for a short while, as if they really belong. The answer is to book an afternoon tea. This is a great tradition of the grandest hotels, which is conducted with the utmost elegance and the minimum of haste. You can relax in the comfort of the sumptuous lounges drinking tea from the best bone china, nibbling on dainty sandwiches and indulging in delicious cakes and pastries which have been freshly cooked by the best pâtissiers in town.

The luxurious Dorchester Hotel in Park Lane is rightly popular with guests who expect first-class comfort and service

# The Wallace Collection

OPPOSITE In addition to paintings and
furniture, the Wallace Collection
contains one of the finest collections of
arms and armour in the world

RIGHT IN THE HEART OF LONDON, JUST NORTH OF Oxford Street, the Wallace Collection is a superb array of Old Masters, sculpture, 18th-century furniture, clocks and objects d'art, porcelain, glass, and miniatures, as well as a substantial arms and armour collection. Despite its merits the collection remains little-visited, which is a bonus for art-lovers, who can enjoy the intimacy of a building that seems more like a private house than a museum. Often the only sounds audible in the carpeted rooms are the tick-tock and tinkling chimes of the fine French clocks.

## AN AVID COLLECTOR

The collection was largely assembled by the 4th Marquess of Hertford, who lived as a recluse in his chateau in the Bois de Boulogne in Paris. Helped by his illegitimate son, Richard Wallace, the Marquess was an avid collector of 18th-century French paintings and furniture, which he bought cheaply in post-Revolutionary France because of their unfashionable (indeed, politically dangerous) associations with the *ancien regime*. The Wallace Collection is especially rich in works by Fragonard, Boucher, Watteau, Lancret and Poussin.

Richard Wallace inherited the collection on his father's death in 1870, moving it to England because of the unstable political situation in France. He added many fine examples of Renaissance ceramics, bronzes, armour and jewellery, and his

widow left the house and the collection to the nation in 1897, on condition that it remained intact. The rooms are packed with all kinds of objects – everything from wall lights and firescreens originally made for the palaces of Fontainebleau and Versailles to 18th-century saucepans and cabinets packed with guns, porcelain or bejewelled baubles.

## THE PAINTINGS

The paintings generally make the most impact, especially Frans Hals' *The Laughing Cavalier* (1624), displayed in the Big Gallery. The unidentified subject wears an almost arrogant smirk beneath his carefully combed moustache, the sense of swagger emphasised by the hand on the hip and the rich lace collar. Here also is a touching portrait by Rembrandt of his son Titus (c1657), the beautiful *Lady with a Fan* by Velazquez and Rubens' *Rainbow Landscape* (c1636). Among the many other highlights, the festive paintings of Fragonard, Lancret and Watteau are full of strange charm, and there are also strong portraits by Gainsborough and Reynolds.

## HERTFORD HOUSE

The house containing the Wallace Collection is deserving of study in its own right. It was built in 1777 for the Duke of Manchester and acquired by the 2nd Marquess of Hertford in 1797. His flamboyant son, the 3rd Marquess, collected many of the 17th-century Dutch paintings in the collection and was able to do so because of his wife's wealth. She was illegitimate – more often than not a barrier to fortune, but in this case two very rich men (the Duke of Queensberry and George Selwyn) claimed to be her father and both left her vast sums of money.

The house was refurnished when Richard Wallace moved the collection here. An important feature is the opulent white marble staircase, made of wrought iron and bronze in 1723–41 for Louis XV and flanked by a magnificent balustrade, It was originally installed in the Palais Mazarin (now the Bibliothèque Nationale) in Paris, and was acquired by Wallace when it was sold for scrap in the chaotic world of mid-19th century Paris.

RIGHT The elegant rooms of Hertford
House host the extensive collection of
the Marquess of Hertford and his son
Richard Wallace

# Temple

ABOVE *Temple Church features an intriguing collection of effigies of 12th- and 13th-century Knights Templars, carved from Purbeck marble*

HE TEMPLE TAKES ITS NAME FROM THE KNIGHTS Templar, the crusading order whose 12th-century round church survives at the heart of this network of alleys and courtyards.

## INNS OF COURT

The Temple actually consists of two Inns of Court (the Inner Temple and the Middle Temple), but they are so physically intertwined as to seem like one large collegiate campus, where lawyers in black gowns stroll between their chambers and the Royal Court of Justice, on the opposite side of Fleet Street. Between the Temple and the Royal Court, in the middle of Fleet Street, is the Temple Bar Memorial, marking the boundary between Westminster and the City.

RIGHT *The 12th-century Temple Church was added to at several periods and restored in 1945–8 after extensive war damage*

Erected in 1880, it is topped by a bronze griffin (the symbol of the city) and is far less imposing than Sir Christopher Wren's gateway, which originally stood here. The gateway was built in 1672 but became an impediment to traffic, and was taken down in 1878.

## THE TEMPLE CHURCH

Just west of the Memorial is a timber-framed gatehouse that leads from busy Fleet Street into the calm of Inner Temple Lane. This leads down to the Temple Church, past the elaborately carved Romanesque west door which is no longer used; the entrance is now from the south. The Temple Church's circular nave, to the left, is known as 'the Round'. It was completed in 1185 and, in common with all the churches built by the Knights Templar, the shape is modelled on the Church of the Holy Sepulchre in Jerusalem. A remarkable series of effigies is set into the floor of the Round: these

### LAWYERS' HAUNTS
◆

The Wig and Pen (Dining) Club, in the Strand, is a favourite haunt for off-duty barristers. With its political and legal cartoons in the window, it is set in a tiny timber-framed building of 1625, the only one on the Strand to have survived the Great Fire of London. Near by, the Law Courts' Branch of Lloyd's Bank has a surprisingly ornate interior — Egyptian-style tiles cover the entrance lobby, and the banking hall is decorated with Doulton tile pictures of flowers, cherubs and historical figures under stucco-work ceilings. All this dates from around 1883 when the building, originally a restaurant, first opened.

LEFT *The tranquillity of Inner Temple Gardens sloping towards the Thames, is in stark contrast to busy Fleet Street, site of the Inns of Court and Chancery buildings*

BELOW *Middle Temple Hall*

three-dimensional figures of sleeping knights, dressed in crusading armour, all date from the late 12th and early 13th centuries. The chancel, known as 'the Oblong', has the same slender Purbeck marble shafts as the Round, but the style is fully-fledged Early English. Added in 1240, the Oblong has been described as 'one of the most perfectly and classically proportioned buildings of the 13th century in England'.

### THE TEMPLE PRECINCTS
Beyond the pretty Master's House, King's Bench Walk is an open space which has unfortunately been spoiled by its use as a car park. To the right, in Crown Office Row, is another leafy garden, but this one is strictly for the use of members of the Temple. An archway links Crown Office Row to the cobbled alley of Middle Temple Lane.

Fountain Court has a huge plane tree and an ancient mulberry, both of which dwarf the tiny circular fountain, and from here, steps lead up to New Court, flanked by ornate gas lamps which are topped by the lamb and flag symbol of the Middle Temple. Beyond the steps an archway leads into Essex Court, then Middle Temple Lane, where there is a delightful row of 17th-century timber framed (but plastered) buildings, whose jettied-out upper storey forms a covered arcade at pavement level.

### MIDDLE TEMPLE HALL
Middle Temple Hall, said to have been opened by Queen Elizabeth I in 1576, has one of the finest hammerbeam roofs in England. Just as spectacular is the Elizabethan oak screen at the east end, carved with big bold figures and statues in niches. The serving table, according to legend, is made from the timbers of Sir Francis Drake's ship, the *Golden Hind*. In this room William Shakespeare took part in a performance of his own *Twelfth Night* on 2 February 1601.

# Lincoln's Inn

LINCOLN'S INN, WHICH HAS THE FINEST GARDENS OF any of the medieval Inns of Court, was possibly named after either the contemporary Earl of Lincoln or a prominent lawyer of the time, Thomas de Lincoln.

On Chancery Lane is the brick gatehouse, dating from 1518 and bearing Henry VIII's coat of arms above original stout oak doorways. The narrow pedestrian entrance leads to the Old Buildings. To the right is the chapel and its stone vaulted undercroft, paved with 18th-century tombstones, and steps lead up from here to the chapel itself, completed in 1623; the poet John Donne preached 'a right rare and learned sermon' at its consecration. The east window contains 228 coats of arms of former Treasurers of Lincoln's Inn. To the right is Old Square, leading to Stone Buildings, built of crisp, white Portland stone in Palladian style. A low gate to the left leads to Lincoln's Inn Fields, a large green area of manicured lawns and statuesque trees. Straight ahead are the hall and library looking perfectly medieval, but built by Philip Hardwick as recently as 1845.

To the left is New Square, where fig trees and wisteria clamber over the late-17th century buildings. Along the left-hand side is Lincoln's Inn Archway, sandwiched between the windows of Wildy & Sons, booksellers specialising in legal texts. The windows exhibit fascinating Victorian cartoons, engravings and cigarette-card views of the Inns of Court. The archway leads into Carey Street, once the site of the bankruptcy courts – hence the expression 'heading for Queer Street' (Queer being a corruption of Carey) to describe someone who is in deep financial trouble.

## Sir John Soane's Museum

This strange but fascinating museum pays tribute to Sir John Soane (1753–1837) – one of those brilliant architects that Britain produces from time to time whose buildings are so quirky and original that they defy classification. Examples of his work in London include the Bank of England, the Dulwich College Picture Gallery and this remarkable house. The house was originally two – he bought No 13 in 1812 and its neighbour No 14 in 1824 and remodelled the interiors to serve as his home and as a museum for his paintings, sculpture, architectural models and drawings (the museum has been extended further by the purchase of No 12, which has been converted to form a gallery for displaying drawings from Soane's massive collection of over 30,000 items).

Soane's interior remodelling was brave and experimental: split-level flooring creates a strange disorienting effect and anticipates, by 100 years or more, a favourite device of modernist architects. The rooms are crammed with objects and made even more bewildering by the use of mirrors. Specially interesting is the Picture Room, housing two of Hogarth's series of paintings. *A Rake's Progress* (1732–3) traces the career of Tom Rakewell in eight canvases, from his life as a carefree young man town to his imprisonment for debt and final home in the Bedlam mad house. *The Election* (c1754) presents an equally cynical view of bribery and corruption in British politics illustrated in four pictures.

The basement resembles a horror movie set, with views through the windows to the Monk's Cloister, built from architectural fragments that Soane rescued when the Houses of Parliament were being rebuilt. Another star exhibit is the Sepulchral Chamber containing the Sarcophagus of Seti I (died c1300 BC), discovered at Thebes in 1817 and offered to the British Museum. When they declined it, Soane bought it and held a three-day long party to celebrate his acquisition.

OPPOSITE *The elegant New Square was completed c1690 before it was part of Lincoln's Inn, while Lincoln's Inn Chapel, right, was rebuilt in the early 17th century*

Sir John Soane's Museum is filled
with his collection of over 30,000
items displayed in a split-level
building of immense character

# ·EAST LONDON·

This is where the oldest and some of the newest parts of London come together, from a section of *Londinium's* Roman wall to the modern development of the old docklands. Between them — geographically and chronologically — are the traditional institutions of the world of finance in the square mile known as The City, with the Bank of England as its nucleus. Clustered around it is a concentration of banks, finance houses, brokers, insurance companies and the high-rise world of high finance.

The legal profession also has its headquarters here, in the cloistered atmosphere of the Inns of Court and the less hallowed halls of the Central Criminial Court.

While the City is constantly looking ahead, the past is not forgotten. There are reminders all around in the street names — Cheapside, for instance, gets its name from the medieval market which was held here. And every November the newly elected Lord Mayor parades through the streets in a fairy-tale horse-drawn carriage accompanied by the kind of pageantry normally reserved for royal occasions. Officials of the ancient trade guilds, or livery companies, bring out their colourful historic costumes and a hundred or more floats follow, attended by bands, cavalry, pikemen and entertainers.

Along the River Thames is London's docklands, which has risen phoenix-like over the last two decades. Extremely disreputable in Victorian times and sadly depressed after the closure of the docks, this area has become an exclusive place to live, with luxury riverside apartments, and is a showcase for modern architecture.

Further east, Greenwich has a more noble maritime heritage which forms one of the most magnificent riverscapes in the world — the superb buildings of the Royal Naval College and National Maritime Museum. This is, of course, site of the Greenwich Meridian at o degrees longitude, marking the division between the eastern and western hemispheres.

*The 'Great Bells of Bow' in St Mary-le-Bow church were sent crashing by a bomb in 1941, only to be recast and rehung in 1962*

# St Paul's Cathedral

*The magificent dome of St Paul's above the Whispering Gallery is decorated with frescos of the life of St Paul, by Sir James Thornhill*

St Paul's Cathedral is one of London's most awe-inspiring sights. Its dome is the third largest in the world and its graceful bulk is an important feature of the City skyline. The building also manages to communicate a sense of serenity, most notably in the famous but fabricated image of 1941 of the dome untouched but wreathed in the smoke and flames of the Blitz. This montage symbolised the undaunted spirit of Londoners during the darkest moments of the war and carried echoes of the cathedral's origins – born out of the flames of the Great Fire of London in 1666.

## SIR CHRISTOPHER WREN

Wren's original design for rebuilding St Paul's was based on High Renaissance ideas, but it was considered too Italianate and too modern – the clergy of St Paul's wanted a traditional processional nave and sanctuary, rather than Wren's Greek Cross design. Wren adapted his plans, but kept the dome which gives the cathedral such a wonderfully uplifting atmosphere. The marvellous choir stalls and organ case near John Donne's tomb were carved by Grinling Gibbons as part of Wren's original decorative scheme.

On entering the church visitors are naturally drawn to the crossing beneath the dome, through whose windows a strangely ambiguous golden light is filtered. In the pavement below its very centre is a memorial to Wren, composed by his son, which reads *Si monumentum requiris, circumspice* – 'If you are seeking his monument, look around you'. Wren's actual tomb – a simple black slab – is in the crypt.

Wren did not want his masterpiece cluttered with memorials, but its symbolic importance made this inevitable. One of the most imposing memorials is to the Duke of Wellington, on the north side of the nave – a huge 'four poster' topped by an equestrian statue. On the opposite side hangs *The Light of the World*, a much-loved painting by Holman Hunt. The tomb of the poet John Donne, on the south side of the choir, shows Donne wrapped in his shroud, and this was the only monument to survive the fire that destroyed the medieval cathedral.

St Paul 's Cathedral at dusk still
conveys the serenity which was an
uplifting symbol for Londoners
during the Blitz

## The Crypt

The crypt is massive, extending beneath nearly the whole of the church. In Painters' Corner, the monuments read like a roll-call of great artists, from Van Dyck to Constable. George Frampton's memorial is particularly charming – it features a small replica of the Peter Pan statue he made for Kensington Gardens. In the centre of the crypt are the tomb of Wellington and the sarcophagus of Nelson. The coffin was made by Benedetto da Rovezzano originally for Cardinal Wolsey, then confiscated by Henry VIII but never used by him. It remained empty until 1805, when Nelson's body was laid to rest within it, having been brought back from the Battle of Trafalgar preserved in spirits. At the west end of the crypt is Wren's 'Great Model', a scale model in wood of the architect's original design.

## The Dome

There are 259 steps leading up to the Whispering Gallery, a circular chamber that carries sound round so that someone standing on the opposite side will hear your whispers quite clearly after several seconds' delay – though with so many visitors testing the acoustics it may be difficult to distinguish any particular message. Views take in the nave below and the frescos of the dome above, depicting scenes from the Life of St Paul painted by Sir James Thornhill in 1716–19.

The Stone Gallery continues around the exterior of the base of the dome, climbing higher to pass through the timberwork that rests on the inner dome, supporting the wooden skin of the outer, lead-covered dome. Between these two domes is a third – the brick cone supporting the elegant lantern which crowns the whole structure, and this can be viewed from the Golden Gallery. There is one last stairway up to the ball, added in 1721, surmounted by a golden cross and looking over the city from 366ft (111m) above the ground. A hole in the floor of the Golden Gallery gives the view straight down to the cathedral floor.

## Around St Paul's

Although the cathedral miraculously escaped major damage in the Blitz, the surrounding area was flattened, then redeveloped in the 1960s with a series of dreary, windswept buildings. These range from the highly modernistic (accused of being out of sympathy with Wren's masterpiece) to the more traditional (accused of being backward-looking), based on Wren's plan to surround his church with Italianate piazzas and boulevards. Most Londoners favour the latter approach, which will give St Paul's the setting it deserves and open up views of the façades. On the south façade Wren had the word *Resurgam* ('I shall rise again') carved above the door and a phoenix rising from the fire carved in the pediment, symbolising the birth of the new church from the ashes of the old. The main (west) façade is the most richly decorated. The baroque twin towers, flanking rows of gigantic columns, are a quirky but successful piece of design to which Wren's gifted pupil Nicholas Hawksmoor may well have contributed.

*The chancel of St Paul's Cathedral – Grinling Gibbons was commissioned to carve the choir stalls, screen and organ case, the vaulting was decorated with coloured glass mosaics by Sir William Richmond*

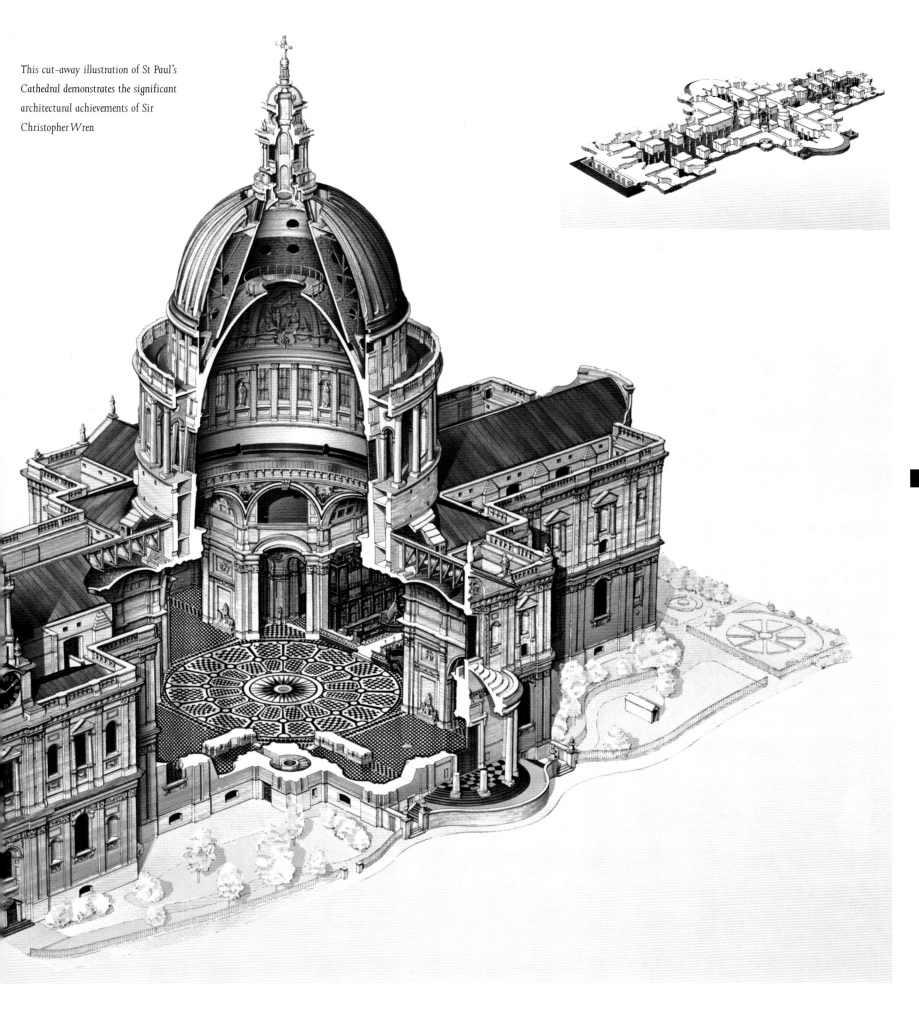

This cut-away illustration of St Paul's Cathedral demonstrates the significant architectural achievements of Sir Christopher Wren

# The City

*Solemn statues adorn the Bank of England building in Threadneedle Street, the financial heart of London, known as the Square Mile*

ONDONERS OFTEN REFER TO THE CITY AS 'THE SQUARE Mile', a name that emphasises how small it is in area, by contrast with its enormous role in the nation's affairs. It was here that London began, founded by the Romans as the administrative capital of *Britannia*. London has since grown to many times its original size, but The City, at its heart, has retained a distinctive identity, with its own police force and its own local authority – the Corporation of London – presided over by the Lord Mayor.

## BANK AND THREADNEEDLE STREET

Bank is to The City what Trafalgar Square is to the West End: a chaotic junction of several roads, surrounded by magnificent public buildings. At the weekend the streets are deserted, but during the week you can stand on any corner at Bank and feel the pulse of this whizz-kid world of high finance and commerce as dealers, messengers and brokers rush between their offices and the main financial markets.

On the north side of Bank is the vast bulk of the Bank of England, after which this whole area is named. The building resembles nothing so much as a fortress – at street level there are no doors or windows in the massive stone walls, except for the main entrance. Sir John Soane designed it to reinforce the idea of rock-solid security, for the Bank's role has always been central to the British economy. The Bank is responsible for issuing banknotes, raising funds for the government, managing the nation's foreign exchange reserves, setting interest rates and regulating the banking system of the country as a whole. The story of its work is told in an excellent museum with high-tech displays that keep track, minute by minute, of all the international money markets.

Further down Threadneedle Street, Old Broad Street leads left to the Stock Exchange. Little did anyone suspect, when this building opened in 1972, that 20 years later it would be all but redundant. The dealing floor, where jobbers traded shares in an atmosphere of tense excitement, lies empty, since buying and selling is now done by telephone and computer in the offices of broking firms.

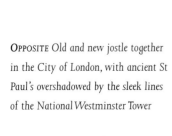

*OPPOSITE Old and new jostle together in the City of London, with ancient St Paul's overshadowed by the sleek lines of the National Westminster Tower*

The Lloyd's Building designed by
Richard Rogers, with detail (inset),
is an enigmatic, futuristic and
ultimately fascinating construction

108

## LLOYD'S OF LONDON

The Lloyd's building, completed in 1986, is one of London's most exciting and controversial modern buildings. Designed by Richard Rogers (who also designed the Pompidou Centre in Paris), it is a daring building all of glass entwined in steel ventilation shafts, cranes, gantries, service pods and staircases. The building is especially thrilling to see at night, when it glows a strange green and purple from concealed coloured spotlights, creating a space-age effect.

Ironically, this forward-looking building houses one of London's most traditional institutions. Lloyd's evolved in the 1680s as a marine insurance market based at Edward Lloyd's Coffee House in Tower Street.

## GUILDHALL

The Guildhall was built in 1411 and despite severe damage during the 1666 Great Fire and the Blitz, its stout medieval walls and impressive undercroft have survived intact. The roof was carefully reconstructed with stone arches by Sir Giles Gilbert Scott in the 1950s. The stained-glass windows incorporate the names of over 600 past Lord Mayors, and the walls and roof are decorated with the coats of arms and embroidered banners of the City Livery Companies. These are the modern equivalent of the medieval trade guilds, who built the Guildhall for their meetings and ceremonies.

The guilds were a powerful force in medieval London, responsible for fixing prices and wages and guaranteeing themselves a monopoly over trade by preventing non-members from setting up shops. Today the Livery Companies support the industries they represent (from brewers to weavers) by funding research and education. From their ranks, the Sheriffs and Lord Mayors are chosen to run the

---

### WEEKEND GHOST TOWN

◆

At the weekend the streets of London's financial centre are as still and quiet as those of a ghost town. The resident population of The City can be numbered in the hundreds. Most City residents live in the Barbican complex and are wealthy enough to afford second homes in the country. When they disappear at the weekend, just about the only people left living in The City are the staff of St Bartholomew's hospital, whose lodgings are in the Charterhouse Square area. This is the time to see some of The City's poignant contrasts, such as the horse-drawn brewers' carts delivering barrels of beer to City pubs against a backdrop of modernistic skyscrapers — Whitbread's brewery is in Chiswell Street, and the company still keeps a team of 16 shire horses for their deliveries to several local pubs.

---

City's affairs, and the Guildhall is where they are installed, amid great ceremony. Looking down from the Guildhall's west gallery are two strange figures: Gog and Magog. These giants, carved in limewood, were made in 1953 by David Evans to replace earlier statues destroyed in the Blitz. Figures of Gog and Magog, mythical founders of ancient Albion (Britain), used to be carried in city pageants. Some of the city's extensive art collection is on display here.

*The impressive 15th-century Guildhall, its splendour reflecting the importance of the guilds at that time, is still used for civic events*

*ABOVE Old Bailey, built on the site of infamous Newgate Prison, takes its name from the street on which it stands*

## COURTROOM DRAMAS

◆

Off Ludgate Hill is Old Bailey, synonymous with the Central Criminal Court which stands here. Built in 1900–7 with a dome inspired by the nearby cathedral, it is topped by the figure of Justice, holding a sword and a pair of scales. The public is admitted to the viewing galleries of the tiny courtrooms (18 in all) and the porters on the doors delight in telling visitors which trials are likely to prove the most salacious or entertaining

## THE HOME OF JOURNALISM

Fleet Street is where some of England's earliest printed books were produced in the 1490s, and five centuries later the name of Fleet Street is still synonymous with the publishing industry, even though all the big newspaper companies have moved from their cramped Fleet Street premises to new high-tech offices all over London. There are still many reminders of the street's history. Near the junction of Fetter Lane and Fleet Street, St Dunstan-in-the-West has both a bust of Lord

Northcliffe, founder of the *Daily Mail* newspaper, and a 1586 statue of Queen Elizabeth I, as well as a clock dating from 1671. A little further on is El Vino's, a traditional wine bar that used to be packed with boozy journalists swapping gossip. Another ex-haunt of journalists is Ye Olde Cheshire Cheese, a historic pub that has scarcely changed since it was rebuilt just after the Great Fire in 1666.

Further down the street are the striking façades of the *Daily Telegraph* building (1928) and that of the *Daily Express* (1931), the latter a daring modernist construction of black glass and chrome. Just before the end of Fleet Street, on the right, a narrow lane leads to St Brides, the journalists' church, with its 'wedding cake' spire. Rebuilt by Christopher Wren after the Great Fire, this is one of the most fascinating churches in London, not least for its unusual crypt museum. Here, foundations revealed by excavation in 1952 show how the church is built over the remains of its three predecessors – 15th-century, Norman and Saxon – all overlying a Roman building. Various displays in the crypt cover the history of printing in Fleet Street.

## THE LORD MAYOR

The City of London has its own local government, headed by the Lord Mayor since 1192, when Henry Fitzailwyn was installed. Today the mayor is elected to serve for just one year. The election takes place on Michaelmas Day, 29 September, and the mayor is installed in the Guildhall on the Friday preceding the second Saturday in November. The next day the mayor drives through the streets, leading the Lord Mayor's Show, a colourful pageant with lavish floats. At the Lord Mayor's Banquet, on the following Monday, the Prime Minister makes an important speech on government policy. Much of the rest of the year is spent attending ceremonial events to raise funds for charity.

## MANSION HOUSE

The official residence of the Lord Mayor of London, the Mansion House is another classical monument (built in 1739–52), whose pediment carvings show London trampling on the figure of Envy (in other words, commercial competitors) and leading in the figure of Plenty. To the west, the triangular plot on the corner of Poultry and Queen Victoria Street is being redeveloped. Controversially, the Flemish Gothic Mappin & Webb building (1870) that stood on the site was demolished in 1994. The much-loved former jeweller's shop is to be replaced by a more modern building whose design, by the late James Stirling, was dismissed by that influential architectural critic, the Prince of Wales, as resembling 'a 1930s wireless set'.

111

*ABOVE The Lord Mayor's Parade is a popular annual attraction, with floats, bands and historical societies attracting large crowds to the area*

*RIGHT St Bride's church was built over three earlier constructions, and is renown for its unusual crypt museum*

# The Barbican Centre

OPPOSITE *The inner sanctums of the Barbican's residential areas are a tranquil haven in contrast to the stark concrete surroundings and bustle all around*

THE BARBICAN CENTRE IS ONE OF LONDON'S MOST important arts venues. The complex serves as home to the London Symphony Orchestra and the London home to the Royal Shakespeare Company, and its programme of events includes a good variety of concerts, exhibitions and film seasons. Quite apart from all this there is a full programme of free foyer exhibitions and musical entertainment, weekend activities especially for children, and an excellent bookshop specialising in the arts.

## LIVING AT THE BARBICAN

The Centre stands on the northern edge of a massive housing complex which is an important example of post-war planning. In 1956, the government proposed that the area, rendered a wasteland by the Blitz, should be developed for housing rather than as office blocks. The architects, Chamberlain, Powell and Bon, produced a scheme which was very forward-looking in its use of textured concrete.

Some 6,500 people now live in the Barbican (which was not finally completed until 1981), many in tower blocks over 400ft (122m) high. Sadly, the buildings are beginning to show their age. The concrete cladding has become stained and dirty, and it is difficult now to visualise how enchanting and futuristic the complex looked when it first opened, with tier upon tier of cascading plants and bright crimson trailing geraniums spilling over every balcony, softening the brutal outlines of the concrete.

*The London home of the Royal Shakespeare Company and the base for the London Symphony Orchestra, the Barbican is a major arts venue*

Most residents have simply given up gardening, partly because of the winds, and partly because so many of them are temporary residents – highly paid media personalities and business executives, for whom this may be only one of many homes. This gives a certain forlorn, unloved atmosphere to the complex, though the area immediately round the arts centre is enlivened by sculptures, water gardens, fountains and trees. The best spots to view the Barbican are from the Waterside Café or the plant-filled conservatory.

## THE BARBICAN MAZE

It is a standing joke among Londoners that once you penetrate the Barbican complex you may never get out. The various buildings are linked by a confusing maze of tunnels, elevated walkways and staircases in which it is all too easy to get lost. To improve the situation, yellow markers have been placed on the pavements, leading eventually to the Barbican Centre arts complex. Alternatively you can use the church of St Giles, Cripplegate for orientation. This Tudor church was left a roofless ruin by the bombing that flattened the surrounding district, but was rebuilt in 1952–60. Surrounded by water, it appears to float on its own island, detached from the massive concrete structures all around. Inside are memorials to people associated with the church: a bust of John Milton, author of *Paradise Lost*, marks the approximate position of his grave. South of the church are remains of London's Roman and medieval city walls.

## THE MUSEUM OF LONDON

This entertaining museum traces the history of London from Roman times to the 20th century through a series of imaginative displays. The first gallery, devoted to the archaeology of London, sets the tone with its reconstructions. One display shows a cross-section of a London street. Evidence of the Great Fire of 1666 is plain to see: a thick layer of charred wood and black ash that still lies below the ground in many parts of London, providing archaeologists with an important benchmark for dating even earlier features.

114

*The cascading plants in the conservatory show how planners visualised the Barbican, but many gardens are now untended*

*One of the Museum of London's most popular exhibits features depictions of Mithras, the invading Roman army's cult god of heavenly light*

Another reconstruction uses fragments of masonry to show what the Roman city's monumental arch would have looked like. These fragments reveal the happy accidents that can occur when ancient remains are investigated. They were found during excavations in 1974–5 which uncovered a substantial length of the Roman wall. On close examination, some of the stones used in building the ramparts were discovered to have carving on their underside, depicting Mars and Mercury. By piecing them together it became apparent that they had come from a late 2nd- or 3rd-century arch, demolished in the 4th century, in the face of crisis, and used to heighten the walls. A section of that 4th-century wall is cleverly revealed as you follow the museum route: just beyond the reconstructed arch is a great glass window that overlooks the remains of the wall in the garden outside. Life in Roman London is illustrated with all kinds of everyday objects – there is even a pair of little leather bikini trunks that were found at the bottom of a 1st-century London well.

## RECENT HISTORY

For many visitors the best of the museum's displays are in the basement and cover more recent London history – shop interiors, kitchen furnishings and toys. Children love

exploring the dank depths of a 1940s' air-raid shelter or the reconstructions of dismal Georgian prison cells, complete with the graffiti scratched by inmates.

Altogether much less chilling are the 18th- and 19th-century costumes, dolls' houses and Valentine's Day cards. The growth of the suburbs is illustrated by 1930s' posters

extolling the newly built housing estates in the rural-sounding Golders Green and Hampstead Garden City. Finally, situated near the exit, where it can be taken out more easily for ceremonial occasions, is the Lord Mayor's state coach, made in 1757 and still used for the Lord Mayor's Show every November. The painted sides of the coach show allegorical scenes set against the background of old London. Other features of the museum include a programme of special events and lectures, and a regular film season, screening films that were made on location in London, from classic Ealing comedies to more recent thrillers. There is also a well-stocked bookshop which sells models and toys.

*Located on London Wall, the Museum of London traces the development of the city through a series of displays, illustrated by archeological finds*

# The East End

*The Bethnal Green Museum of Childhood features an extensive collection of dolls and their houses, re-created in astonishing detail*

*The iron and glass building of the Museum of Childhood was originally part of the Victoria and Albert Museum, designed by Paxton*

THE SCORES OF COMMUNITIES TO THE EAST OF THE CITY each have their own strong identity and are well worth exploring for a different view of London.

## BETHNAL GREEN MUSEUM OF CHILDHOOD

Featuring the largest collection of toys in the world, this museum has plenty to justify the trip out to a rather desolate area of London's East End. The museum is an outpost of the Victoria and Albert Museum and is housed in an iron and glass building that originally stood on the V & A's South Kensington site, but was re-erected here in 1875 and clad in brick with sgraffito (scratched) designs illustrating the Arts, Sciences and Agriculture.

A wonderful collection of 50 doll's houses is on display. Visitors can peer into the miniature world of a grand late-19th century country house, stuffed with heavy furniture, or envy the lifestyle of the tiny inhabitants of Whiteladies, a stylish 1930s modernist house complete with tennis court, swimming pool and veranda for cocktails. The lower galleries house a huge toy collection from all over the world, grouped by type (dolls, trains, teddy bears, optical or musical toys), the earliest exhibits being 17th-century.

The exhibits upstairs illustrate the social history of childhood and exhibits here include children's clothing from the 1830s to the present day, reconstructed nurseries and also books from the museum's vast Renier Collection, covering the way in which subjects as diverse as sex and religion have been presented to children over the last 400 years.

## SPITALFIELDS

A visit to Spitalfields provides the opportunity to sample the surprising contrasts of London's East End. This working-class neighbourhood has long been home to the poorest of refugees. Its character was first formed by Huguenot weavers, whose houses still have skylit attics where hand-loom weavers worked all the hours of daylight to produce fine silk clothing. After the Huguenots came Jewish refugees from Russia and Poland, specialising in furs and leather, only to be followed more recently by Bengali immigrants, who now toil in the same 18th-century buildings over sewing machines and steam irons, producing garments for sale in London's vast selection of clothes shops.

## COVENT GARDEN OF THE EAST

The Spitalfields area begins at Liverpool Street Station, recently restored to its full Victorian splendour, and is now earmarked as the 'Covent Garden of the east', although much work is still to be done, and Christ Church, towering above the eastern end of the market, may eventually become the focal point of the development.

This huge church, which was built in 1714, is Nicholas Hawksmoor's masterpiece; it represents a controversial mixture of classical Renaissance and baroque elements. Long neglected, and even threatened with demolition, it is now used both as a church and as a concert hall. Some of the gravestones in the churchyard have epitaphs in French, marking the graves of Huguenot refugees who found a haven here after the Edict of Nantes, which had guaranteed their right to religious freedom, was revoked in 1685. Some grew wealthy as master weavers in the production of silks, damasks and velvets. Their houses can be seen in Fournier Street, to the north of Christ Church. Built between 1718 and 1728, several have been restored by their owners with an almost exaggerated respect for authenticity.

## A MELTING POT

Brick Lane, at the heart of a large community of Asians from Bangladesh, Pakistan and India, is lined with shops selling exotic groceries and brightly printed fabrics and saris, and the simple restaurants here serve some of the most authentic curries to be found in London. At certain times this whole area seems like one huge street market. At the northern end of Brick Lane, stalls are set up from dawn on Sunday and further south and west, Commercial Street, Wentworth Street and Middlesex Street are crammed with the stalls of Asian, Cockney and Jewish traders at the weekend.

## JACK THE RIPPER

◆

The notorious killer's six
victims were murdered over
an eight-week period
beginning on 7 August 1888,
when the first horribly
mutilated body was found
by a Spitalfields Market
porter in nearby Gunthorpe
Street. The Jack the Ripper
pub, near Christ Church
on Commercial Street, has
a window engraved with the
full list of his victims.
The failure of the police to
find the elusive murderer
led to the resignation of the
London Police Commissioner,
but also to a growing taste
among the public at large for
crime and detective stories,
such as *The Adventures of
Sherlock Holmes*, which Sir
Arthur Conan Doyle began to
pen in 1891.

117

Fournier Street in Spitalfields is
dominated by the vast Christ Church,
designed by Christopher Wren's pupil,
Nicholas Hawksmoor

# Tower Bridge

OWER BRIDGE IS A FANCIFUL STRUCTURE DESIGNED IN Gothic style to complement its neighbour, the Tower of London. Opened with great ceremony in 1894, the only major change since then has been the installation of electrical motors in 1976 to lift the two massive central spans of the drawbridge to allow ships to pass through. Its original steam engines remain as the focal point of a museum entered from the north tower, from where lifts carry visitors up to the footbridge linking the two towers high above the river. The footbridge was built so that pedestrians could continue to use the bridge while the drawbridge was raised below. Now glassed in because of its reputation as a suicide spot, it offers sweeping views over London. The south tower leads to the main part of the museum, which includes the steam-driven hydraulics of the Victorian era, and working models and videos showing how the lifting mechanism works.

## ST KATHARINE DOCK
◆

St Katharine Dock was built in 1824–8 by Thomas Telford and is the closest of all London's docks to the City of London. This proximity to the financial centre made the dock a prime target for redevelopment when it became redundant in 1968, and the 19th-century warehouses have been converted to luxury flats for boat-lovers, whose yachts are moored in one of the two main basins. Mingling among them are historic vessels, including Thames sailing barges which are available for hire (with crew) and the lightship *Norse*, which once operated in the Thames estuary. The dock is a peaceful spot, popular for pub food served at the Dickens Inn, artfully restored from an 18th-century timber-framed brewery that was discovered incorporated into a warehouse of later date.

*BELOW AND RIGHT Modern yachts and historic craft are moored among the converted warehouses and swing bridges of St Katharine Dock*

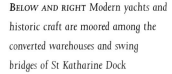

*OPPOSITE Tower Bridge by night is impressive enough, but few sights can match the spectacle of the bridge raised for the passage of tall ships*

# The Tower of London

*ABOVE Some rather gruesome imagery, designed to instil fear no doubt, adorns this Flemish gun in the confines of the Tower of London*

*RIGHT The Tower's human guardians — the Yeoman Warders, or Beefeaters as they are commonly known — stand resplendent in their Tudor costumes*

*RIGHT AD 1270: Henry III built a towered stone wall and moat to the north, east and north-west, incorporating the Church of St Peter ad Vincula in the north-west corner, and a landgate on the site of the present Beauchamp Tower. He also completed the southern outer wall. A watergate, later incorporated into the Bloody Tower, gave access to the river. Against this wall he built a Gothic great hall; his keep also included an elephant house, part of the royal menagerie.*

T HE TOWER OF LONDON CAN BE ONE OF THE MOST crowded spots in London in summer, its appeal based on its long and bloody history. Many famous and beautiful heads were parted from their pampered bodies within the confines of this most splendid of fortress-palaces.

## DARK DEEDS

Several dark deeds were committed in the tower. The 'Little Princes', Edward V and his brother Richard, were murdered in the Bloody Tower in 1483, possibly by their uncle, Richard III. But the pace of execution really stepped up under Henry VIII, whose second and fifth wives, Anne Boleyn and Catherine Howard, were executed here. The same fate was in store for Lady Jane Grey, who was proclaimed Queen of England in 1553 but deposed after nine days, and Sir Thomas More and Sir Walter Ralegh were held here as prisoners before their journeys to the scaffold.

The site of the block was on Tower Green, in front of the Chapel of St Peter ad Vincula. In 1870 the floor was raised to reveal a pile of beheaded skeletons, including those of Henry VIII's two unfortunate discarded wives.

Prisoners were brought in and out of the Tower by boat through the Traitor's Gate, still a watergate in the outer wall of the Tower, visible from the embankment. Not surprisingly, the Tower is hailed as the most haunted building in London: the headless body of Anne Boleyn has been seen gliding across Tower Green and Sir Walter Ralegh's ghost walks the ramparts on moonlit nights.

*ABOVE* The Tower of London has defied the ravages of time to stand as a great symbol of strength and continuity for many generations

RIGHT AD **1100**: The White Tower, built to overawe the people of London and control access to the city from the sea, replaced a wooden fort built by the Normans in 1067. Parts of the masonry were retained to the east, but a new stone wall was erected to the north and west. The White Tower was unfinished when William I died in 1087, but was completed by his son William II in about 1097.

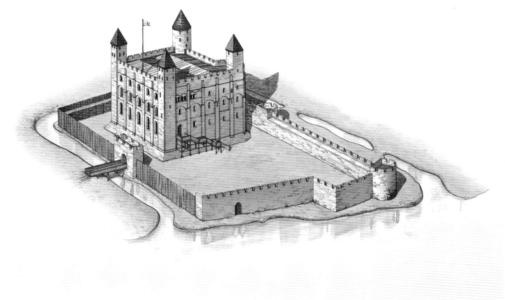

Built originally as a watchtower by
William I, the Tower of London has
developed over the centuries into this
truly imposing fortress

## THE ROYAL PALACE

Of course, the Tower was not just a place of torture and execution – it also served as a royal palace. William the Conqueror began its construction in 1078, building the central keep, known as the White Tower because it was whitewashed during the reign of Henry III (1216–72). Henry kept his menagerie here, including three leopards, given to him by the Holy Roman Emperor, and a polar bear, the gift of the King of Norway. The White Tower now houses a museum of arms and armour. However, the displays have undergone some reorganisation and, prompting a degree of controversy, some of the exhibits have been moved to Leeds to offer the rest of the country a chance to appreciate them. In the tower museum a series of suits of armour made for Henry VIII reveal his deterioration from slim youth to massive middle age and the image familiar to many who have seen Holbein's portrait of the ever-expanding monarch.

## THE CROWN JEWELS – AND OTHER TREASURES

The Crown Jewels are kept in the 19th-century Waterloo Barracks, beside the chapel. Most of the jewels date from the period after 1660; earlier regalia were melted down after Charles I's execution in 1649. Queen Victoria's Imperial State Crown has many famous jewels, but none is so well known as the Koh-i-Noor diamond on the Queen Mother's crown.

Almost as valuable are the 42 Yeoman Warders who have looked after the tower since their appointment by Henry VII in 1485. They are nicknamed 'Beefeaters' either because they once attended the king's table as 'buffetiers', or because of the meat allowance they received from the Crown. Dressed in Tudor-style uniforms, they conduct tours and are a mine of information about the Tower's history.

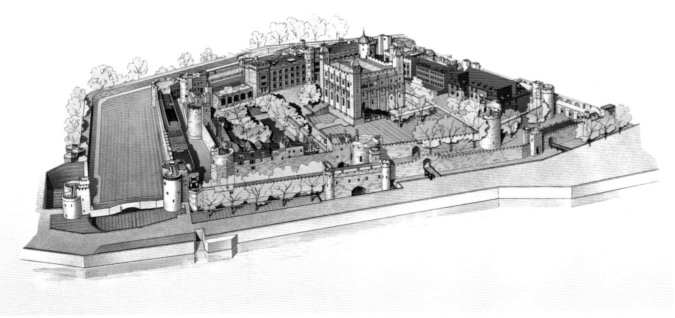

ABOVE *The costumes and the firearms may reflect modern times, but the nightly Ceremony of the Keys is steeped in centuries of tradition*

LEFT *Although treason is still a capital offence in Britain, Traitor's Gate should hold few fears for those passing through it nowadays*

LEFT *1996: Completing the illustrative representations of the Tower of London complex throughout the ages is its modern form. In an attempt to re-create the past, the idea of reconstructing the moat is receiving serious consideration.*

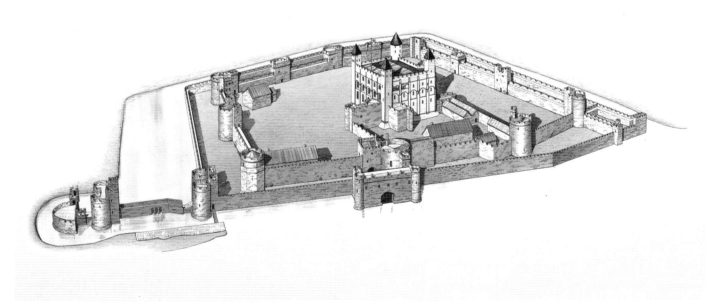

LEFT AD 1300: Henry's son, Edward I, created a new line of outer defences. He filled in his father's moat and gained land from the river to the south to make a narrow Outer Ward surrounded by a peripheral wall, then dug a moat around the entire fortress. He replaced Henry's landgate with the Beauchamp Tower and created a new landward entrance which had an outer barbican (the Lion Gate), a Middle Tower (today's entrance) and the Byward Tower. A new watergate was constructed, St Thomas's Tower where Edward had his private apartments.

# Docklands

*Opposite* The development of the docklands has transformed this part of east London into an area of converted warehouses and luxury apartments

L ONDON'S FORMER DOCKLANDS LIE TO THE EAST OF THE City, covering a vast area, equal in size to the whole of central London. London's post-war decline as a port made great tracts of land available for development, and in the 1980s Docklands was seen by some as a solution to inner-city decline. New apartments, offices and leisure facilities would persuade people to live in London instead of commuting. The docks themselves represented the potential for leisure marinas and water sports. In the event, this transformation has proved much slower than was envisaged, and several developers have ended up bankrupt; there has also been fierce opposition to the policy as a whole. Nevertheless, the area is a source of fascination, with converted warehouses and historic buildings juxtaposed with post-modernist buildings, most famously the Canary Wharf development.

*Shedding part of its rough and ready reputation, this part of east London has benefited from a great deal of regeneration in recent years*

## SHIPYARDS AND OPIUM DENS

◆

Limehouse was one of London's main shipbuilding centres in the 18th and 19th centuries. In the 1890s, Chinese sailors from Hong Kong and Canton set up London's first Chinatown here, notorious for its opium dens and gambling parlours. Names such as Canton Street, Pekin Street and Nankin Street, to the north of East India Dock Road, are a reminder of those times, and there is still a sizeable Chinese population. Limehouse retains its original historic character, and it was one of the first parts of the Docklands to be colonised in the 1980s, when apartments in converted warehouses were the height of fashion. The most attractive buildings are found in Narrow Street, where the locks at Limehouse Basin link a branch of the Grand Union Canal with the Thames. The Grapes pub, in Narrow Street, was immortalised by Dickens in *Our Mutual Friend*, and its restaurant is renowed for fresh fish.

## CANARY WHARF

Canary Wharf is a monument to the optimism of the 1980s, when demand for new office space seemed endless. Existing buildings in the City of London were difficult to adapt to provide the huge open spaces demanded by modern financial trading companies, so developers looked east, to Docklands, a huge site where planning laws were deliberately relaxed to encourage ambitious building schemes.

## THE PLAN FOR A MINI CITY

Canary Wharf certainly was ambitious. The developers, Olympia & York, spent £1¼ billion in constructing a self-contained mini-city, with over a million square metres of office space – enough to present a serious challenge to City landlords, who feared that older buildings in the 'square mile' would be left empty as financial institutions migrated east.

Canary Wharf was to have had four floors of shops, two hotels, exhibition and conference centres, swimming pools, tennis courts and gymnasia, and the principal buildings were to be lined with a series of piazzas, with statues, gardens, fountains, waterside walks and historic ships moored in the adjacent West India Docks basin. Transport will be provided by extending the Jubilee underground line into Docklands.

The whole scheme foundered in 1992 when the developers went into liquidation, but not before the huge 800ft (244m) central tower, known as One Canada Square, had been completed. This massive structure dominates the east and south London skyline, its flashing beacon visible for miles around. Much of the building is empty, although various potential tenants have expressed an interest.

*To visit Docklands take the Docklands Light Railway passing through the heart of the development, or go on a riverboat trip to Greenwich*

# Greenwich

G REENWICH IS EVERY BIT AS BEAUTIFUL AS ITS NAME (a corruption of 'green reach') suggests. Here, set in parkland that sweeps down to the river's edge, are some of London's most noble buildings, including the Queen's House, built by Inigo Jones between 1616 and 1635 and now used to house the National Maritime Museum, and Wren's Royal Naval College alongside the Thames. Together they form one of the most impressive groupings in the whole of London, best viewed from across the river.

## HISTORIC SHIPS

At Greenwich Pie, the *Cutty Sark* lies moored in a dry dock, housing an exhibition of ships' figureheads below deck. This sleek and handsome ship, with its tall masts and intricate rigging, was built in 1869 as a tea clipper, carrying precious cargoes between Britain and the Orient. In 1871 she broke the world record for sailing between London and China, completing the trip in only 107 days, and at her fastest she was covering 360 miles (580km) in a single day. The price of

*A splendid sight from across the Thames, the neo-classical home of the Royal Naval College was originally built as a naval hospital*

The Cutty Sark, with its imposing rigging and familiar figurehead, inset, is a reminder of the tea clippers and cargo ships once built in the area

## MACARTNEY HOUSE

◆

This is one of several elegant 17th- and 18th-century houses lining Croom's Hill, the winding road that links Greenwich village to the Ranger's House on Chesterfield Walk. General Edward Wolfe, who purchased the house in 1751, described it as 'the prettiest situated house in England'. General Edward was the father of the more famous General James Wolfe, who set off from this house in 1758 for North America, at the head of a force which captured Quebec from the French. Wolfe was fatally wounded in the process and a statue of him by Tait Mackenzie (1930), given by the Canadian nation, stands in Greenwich Park, not far from the Royal Observatory. There is also a memorial to him in St Alfege's Church in Greenwich.

this streamlining and speed was the cramped living conditions which were endured by the 28-man crew.

Moored near by, and dwarfed by the magnificent *Cutty Sark*, is *Gipsy Moth IV*, the tiny yacht in which Sir Francis Chichester made the first single-handed circumnavigation of the globe in 1966–7. Nearly 400 years before that, Sir Francis Drake had been the first Englishman to sail round the world. The sword used by Queen Elizabeth II to knight Sir Francis Chichester was the same one used by Elizabeth I to knight Drake back in the 16th century.

## THE ROYAL NAVAL COLLEGE

Splendid wrought-iron gates on King William Walk form the main entrance to the Royal Naval College, now used for officer training, but originally built as a hospital for infirm and aged seamen. These monumental buildings, begun in 1664, stand around the open space of the Great Court. The great architect Sir Christopher Wren planned the symmetrical blocks on either side of the court specifically to frame the impressive southward view of the Queen's House.

The Painted Hall features some of the finest baroque paintings in England, executed by Sir James Thornhill in 1707–17 and featuring the monarchs William and Mary, surrounded by allegorical figures symbolising the triumph of virtue over vice. The Chapel, rebuilt after being damaged by a fire in 1779, is in neo-Grecian style, with statues of Faith, Hope, Charity and Humility in the vestibule and a vast altar painting by Benjamin West, *St Paul Shaking Off the Viper*.

**ABOVE** *The intricate wrought-iron balustrade of the Tulip Stair in the Queen's House mimics the fleurs-de-lis emblem of France*

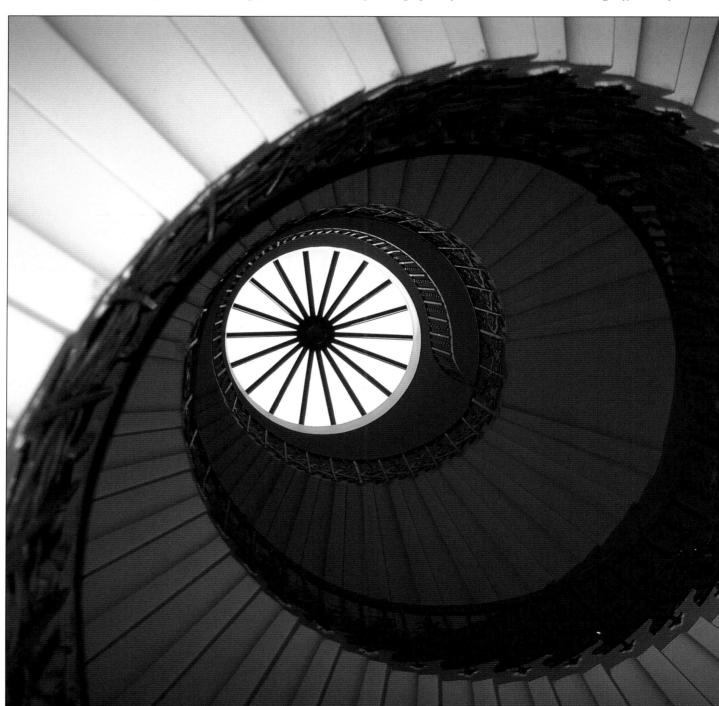

**RIGHT** *The awesome spiral staircase in the Queen's House was designed by Inigo Jones for Queen Anne, who died before its completion*

## NATIONAL MARITIME MUSEUM & QUEEN'S HOUSE

The main attraction in Greenwich is the National Maritime Museum, which occupies several buildings in Greenwich Park and tells the story of Britain and the sea.

The museum's central building, the Queen's House, is an important architectural monument in its own right – the first building in England to be designed in the classical style, and the prototype for many subsequent public buildings and stately homes. Inigo Jones began the building in 1616 as a rural retreat for Anne of Denmark, James I's queen, but she died in 1619 and it was Henrietta Maria, the French wife of Charles I, who presided over its completion in 1635.

The finest feature of the interior is the 'Tulip Stair', named after the pattern on its balustrade (probably intended

to represent fleurs-de-lis, the traditional symbol of France). The staircase leads to the Great Hall, a perfect cube, with ceiling paintings showing the Muses, the Virtues and the Liberal Arts. The original paintings were moved to Marlborough House, Pall Mall, in the 18th century – these are computer-enhanced re-creations.

To either side are the State Apartments (the king's to the east and the queen's to the west), furnished in 17th-century style. One of the most intriguing rooms in the house is the Queen's Presence Chamber, where original painted decorations survive, showing the lilies of France impaling the British arms and symbolising the marriage of Charles I to Henrietta Maria.

The long side wings, added to the Queen's House in 1807–16 to house the Royal Hospital School, now contain a huge collection of ships (real ones and models), paintings, navigational instruments and the relics of naval heroes and explorers. The star attraction is the Neptune Hall, which explains the development of wooden boats from prehistoric times to the present day. The adjacent Barge House contains the state barge, a riot of carved and gilded decoration, made in 1732 for Frederick, Prince of Wales. Other displays tell the story of the explorers who charted the Arctic during the period 1818–76, and of early colonists who braved the Atlantic in search of a new life. In the Nelson Collection visitors can see the uniform jacket, with a bullet-hole in the left shoulder, that Nelson was wearing when he was fatally wounded at the Battle of Trafalgar in 1805.

## THE OLD ROYAL OBSERVATORY

The Old Royal Observatory is an annexe to the Maritime Museum, consisting of several historic buildings, high on the hill above Greenwich. The Greenwich Observatory was

*It is easy to see why the classical elegance of the Queen's House inspired so many similar buildings to be constructed in and around London*

129

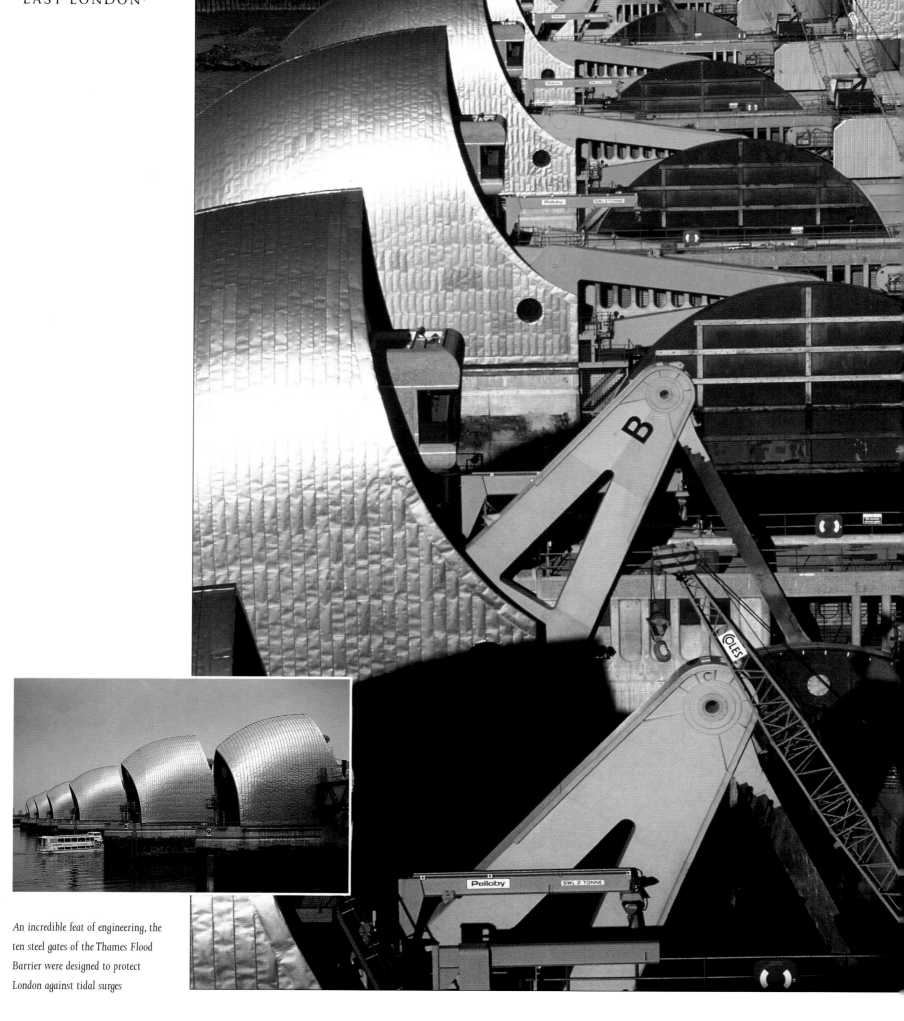

An incredible feat of engineering, the ten steel gates of the Thames Flood Barrier were designed to protect London against tidal surges

founded by Charles II in 1675, and Flamsteed House was built in the same year by Sir Christopher Wren for John Flamsteed (1646–1719), the first Astronomer Royal. The house is decorated to give the impression that Flamsteed and his wife still live there, with food on the table, clothes strewn about and a chamberpot under the bed. Early telescopes and time-measuring instruments are displayed in the house, and the large red ball on top of one of the towers still drops down its mast at 1pm each day, enabling Thames navigators to set their chronometers accurately.

Right from the start, the Observatory's job was to set standards of measurement for time, distance, latitude and longitude – key components of navigation. The large Gate Clock measures Greenwich Mean Time, the standard by which time is set all round the world, and the Greenwich Meridian is marked by a brass strip crossing the Observatory courtyard. It represents the dividing line between the earth's eastern and western hemispheres.

### THE VILLAGE

Immediately south of the pier is College Approach, the route into Greenwich Village, lined with early-19th century buildings, which flank the entrance to Greenwich Market. The covered market, built in 1831, is now only open at weekends and specialises in crafts. Another market, selling antiques, books and period clothing, operates during weekends in the summer on Greenwich Church Street.

The grand 18th-century Ranger's House standing on the edge of Greenwich Park has had many aristocratic residents. Princess Sophie Matilda, daughter of George III lived here from 1814, with the title of Ranger of Greenwich Park. The house is now displays the Dolmetsch Collection of historical musical instruments and the Suffolk Collection of English portraits of the 17th and 18th centuries. This includes a series of paintings by William Larkin of ladies dressed in gorgeous court costumes, commissioned about 1614 to commemorate the marriage of Elizabeth Cecil and Thomas Howard.

*The Royal Observatory offers a computer print-out recording the precise time of any visit to the Greenwich Meridian*

*Flamsteed House was built for Sir John Flamsteed, the first Astronomer Royal, whose data assisted Newton with his theory of gravity*

# ·SOUTH LONDON·

outh London, particularly south of the river, is sometimes looked upon as a kind of poor relation of the rest of the capital — certainly, it has its fair share of run-down areas and featureless suburbs, but there are also real gems for those who are prepared to seek them out.

In a loop of the river, on its north side, are such fashionable areas as Belgravia and Pimlico, while across the river at Bankside there is a cultural enclave in the South Bank arts complex, which includes the National Theatre, the National Film Theatre and the Royal Festival Hall, along with a variety of other arts venues, an art gallery and the highly entertaining Museum of the Moving Image. There are plans to pretty up the whole area, but it is already a pleasant and relaxing place to stroll around, with its lovely riverside walk leading past the reconstructed Globe Theatre and the former Bankside Power Station, which is being converted into a modern art gallery.

Much further south, the 'village' of Dulwich is well worth the journey — one of south London's most attractive suburbs, with beautiful parks and gardens, a famous college and one of the best art collections in the world.

*Part of London Bridge City, Hay's Galleria, a shopping precinct built on Hay's Dock, abounds with glass, steel barrel-vaulting and sculptures*

# The South Bank Centre

ONDON'S SOUTH BANK HAS A LONG ASSOCIATION WITH the theatre. In former times theatres, bearpits and brothels were banned from the City because apprentices spent too much time play-going. The actors promptly moved to the south bank, out of the City's jurisdiction.

## THEATRES AND CONCERT HALLS

Today the south bank is altogether a more salubrious cultural enclave, featuring a cluster of vibrant music and arts venues alongside Waterloo Bridge. The Royal Festival Hall was the first to be built, as the centrepiece of the Festival of Britain in 1951, an event designed to cheer up the population after years of austerity and widespread rationing during World War II. The hall, with seating for 3,000, has two resident orchestras – the London Philharmonic and the Philharmonia – and has excellent acoustics, spacious foyers and fine river views. In the late 1960s, the adjacent Queen Elizabeth Hall, seating 1,000, and the more intimate Purcell Room, with a capacity of just 330, opened. Completing the complex is the

*BELOW AND OPPOSITE Rather dull by daylight, the Royal Festival Hall glitters at night, when concert goers flock to hear the finest classical music*

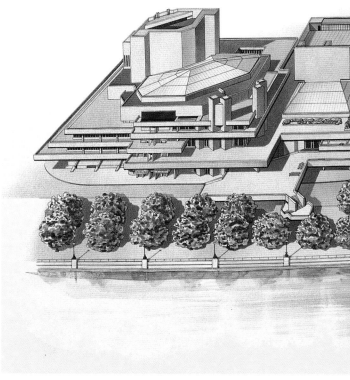

*ABOVE The Hayward Art Gallery was purpose-built to provide a wonderful showcase for its programme of temporary exhibitions of fine art*

Hayward Gallery, which stages important exhibitions, the National Film Theatre, with three cinemas showing the finest selection of new and classic films, and the newest addition, the Museum of the Moving Image.

Close by is The Royal National Theatre, which actually consists of three theatres – the Olivier, the Lyttleton and the Cottesloe, which has flexible seating to suit its programme of

experimental and fringe theatre events. As well as the concerts, plays and exhibitions held in the principal buildings, the foyer spaces and traffic-free riverside terraces are used for free exhibitions, markets and busking.

*RIGHT The National Theatre actually consists of three theatres, where a wide range of British and world drama, classics and new plays are performed*

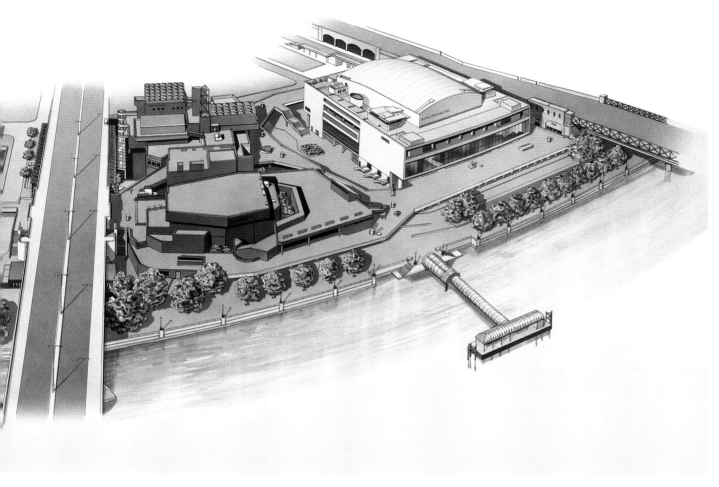

BOTTOM The Museum of the Moving Image is adorned with popular screen icons; below, a praxinoscope gives the illusion of movement

## MUSEUM OF THE MOVING IMAGE

This is a museum about the world of movies, video and television and MOMI, as it is popularly known, really does provide an entertaining look at the world of entertainment. Much of its success is due to the staff of actor-guides, who really bring the world of the big and small screen to life. Some appear in the guise of famous movie and television stars, such as the Charlie Chaplin lookalike, performing in narrative, mime and improvisation to tell the story of the silent screen; other characters will involve visitors in auditions, putting them through their paces, maybe for a place in the chorus of a Hollywood musical.

Participation is an integral part of the museum, and visitors can read the news, help to make an animated cartoon, be a chat-show guest and even fly like Superman! Children can take part in shows, and there are lots of inter-active displays. No-one who suffers from stage-fright is thrust into the spotlight, though, and there are a huge number of exhibits to enjoy without taking part.

The world of the moving image is not as recent as some of us may believe, and the museum tells the history of the Javanese shadow theatre that originated some 4,000 years ago. Mostly, though, it is the nostalgia of the images of living memory that appeal. Exhibits are enlivened by the use of stills, old newsreels, advertisements and film clips, and there are special displays on such subjects as the films of Alfred Hitchcock and Sergei Eisenstein, the Hollywood Dream Factory and wartime film-making.

The serious side of the media is covered in sections devoted to censorship, to the challenges involved in making objective documentary programmes and to such themes as the contribution of the avant-garde or German Expressionism to modern cinematic ideas.

The museum also has its own big screen cinema, showing a varied programme of films. Even here the museum's penchant for theatrical presentation creeps in, in the form of a doorman and usherette dressed in the costumes of the cinema's heyday, swapping quips which were first heard on the lips of Mae West and Humphrey Bogart.

The long-awaited reconstruction of the Globe Theatre recalls a time when a visit to the theatre was a far cry from the hushed, respectful event it is today

This detail from the Globe Theatre shows the craftsmanship and attention to historic building techniques that have gone into its reconstruction

*The London Dungeon is the perfect antidote for visitors who have over-dosed on the more aesthetically pleasing cultural attractions of London*

Athough the great windowless concrete edifices of the South Bank Complex were highly regarded by the world of architecture, they have never found much favour with the public, who generally find the weather-stained, tired looking concrete ugly and cheerless. However, much has been done to improve the look of the area around the complex, with a lovely riverside walk and the Jubilee Gardens.

## THE GLOBE THEATRE

A little further along the river from the South Bank Centre is the recently opened replica of Shakespeare's original Globe Theatre, the brainchild of Sam Wanamaker (1919–93), the American film and theatre director.

No area of London was rougher than Southwark when Shakespeare's original Globe Theatre was built here in 1598–9. In a region surrounded by brothels, taverns, bear pits and cock pits, it enabled the apprentices of the day to come to the theatre instead for their entertainment. The progress of the replica was followed avidly and visitors could watch the building taking shape, a painstaking exercise using late-16th century construction techniques. The rim of the building has been constructed using authentic materials, including a thatched roof, while the centre remains unroofed, and open-air productions will be held here. Surrounding the theatre is an educational and cultural complex where displays trace the history of Southwark's notorious entertainment district.

## LONDON DUNGEON

◆

Gruesome is the only word to describe the London Dungeon, which is definitely not for the faint hearted and yet is among the most popular attractions in London. For those who like to have their spines well and truly chilled, there could be nowhere better, and children in particular seem to delight in the horrific sights presented in this series of slimy vaults along the river past Southwark Bridge. The seamy and sadistic side of life in past centuries is convincingly re-created, including realistic portrayals of executions and torture – martyrdom, hanging, flogging, boiling alive, burning at the stake and disembowelling.

The tools of witchcraft and black magic are displayed, and because early medicinal practises were equally grisly, they have not been overlooked.

The latest in interactive technology is utilised to its full advantage in the 'Theatre of the Guillotine' and in the 'Jack the Ripper Show', a tour around Victorian Whitechapel.

The most appalling feature of this hugely successful attraction is that nearly every display is based on reality, simply reflecting the extraordinarily cruel punishments that human beings have devised and inflicted upon their agonised victims in the past. Children can enjoy the spectacle because they know 'it is not real', whereas adults know only too well that it is.

# The Imperial War Museum

W HEREAS MOST THEMED MUSEUMS ARE A CELEBRATION of their subject, the Imperial War Museum sets out not to glorify war, but to represent it in a thought-provoking way. The result is one of London's most impressive and effective museums, covering the two World Wars and other post-1914 British military operations.

Vivid re-creations bring home the horrors of conflict in a number of scenarios, including the walk-through Trench Experience and a simulated Royal Air Force bombing raid. The Blitz Experience consists of a street scene from bombed-out London, with the rubble of collapsed, fire-gutted buildings, the acrid smells of charred wood and the eerie sound of air-raid sirens, illustrating what it was like to live through the war on the home front.

The fighting fronts of Europe, Africa and the Far East are also depicted, with excellent use made of audio-visual and documentary film footage, while other exhibits remind us of the horrors of the concentration camps.

On the ground floor is the impressive collection of military hardware, exploring the mechanical and technical aspects of 20th-century warfare. There are enormous tanks

## BEDLAM

◆

The fine classical building that houses the Imperial War Museum was formerly the Bethlehem Royal Hospital, an asylum for the mentally ill popularly known as Bedlam. The hospital moved here in 1816 as part of a general improvement in standards. Prior to this, in its Moorfields location, the patients were cruelly treated and were displayed in caged cells, like animals in a zoo, for the flocks of visitors who would come to look at them. It was not until the late 18th century that the cruelty of such treatment was appreciated — the fact that George III suffered mental illness helped to bring about a more humane attitude. Criminal patients were moved from here to Broadmoor in 1864 and in 1930 the remaining patients were moved to new premises in Surrey.

*Although the social impact of 20th-century warfare is the focus of this splendid museum, it also has collections of tanks and weapons*

142

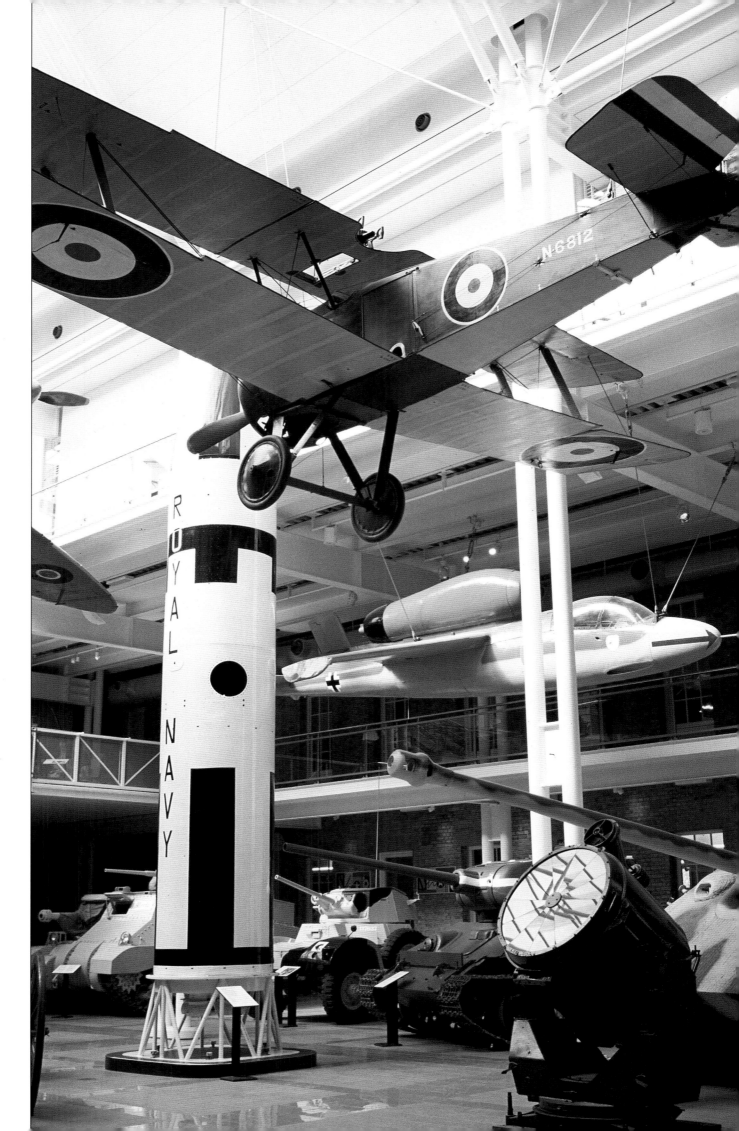

*A fascinating range of military hardware is on display, from the fragile-looking biplanes of the early days of flying, to modern missiles*

from Britain, the USA and Russia, military aircraft, missiles (including the infamous German v2 rocket), artillery, giant naval guns and even an early submarine. Aerial warfare is the theme of the first-floor gallery, which also includes some of the weapons captured from the Argentinians during the Falklands Campaign of 1982.

## WAR ART

The human side of war is conveyed through the recorded words of war poets and the vivid pictures and sculptures of artists such as David Bomberg, Carel Weight, Henry Moore, John Piper, Sir Stanley Spencer, Orpen, Paul Nash, Henry Moore, Graham Sutherland, Edward Burra and many more. The insidious weapons of germ and chemical warfare are represented by John Singer Sargent's large and nightmarish picture of 1918–19, simply entitled *Gassed*.

The top floor of the museum is devoted to works of art by official war artists, including some of the most important painters and sculptors of our time. The theme of war and the recreation of a brave new post-war world are conveyed in the fractured works of Wyndham Lewis, studies of the Clyde shipbuilding yards by Stanley Spencer and by Sir Jacob Epstein's forceful head of Sir Winston Churchill.

*Among the evocative works of art on display at the museum is Take Off by Dame Lenra Knight, painted during World War II*

143

## HMS BELFAST

An outpost of the Imperial War Museum moored on the Thames, HMS *Belfast*, is one of the largest warships ever built for the British Navy. She was launched just before World War II, but on 21 November 1939 she was almost destroyed by a German magnetic mine and had to undergo substantially rebuilding. She then played an important part in the D-Day landings of June 1944, as one of the ship's several small exhibitions reveals.

*Visitors to HMS Belfast, a floating annexe of the museum, can clamber all over the ship, from the bridge and gun turrets to the boiler room*

# Dulwich

THIS HIGHLY CIVILISED SUBURB IS KNOWN FOR ITS WIDE open spaces, notable art gallery and famous school, but in medieval times Dulwich was just a hamlet owned by Bermondsey Abbey. Its fortunes began to change in 1605, when the entire manor was bought by actor-manager Edward Alleyn, a friend of Christopher Marlowe.

## DULWICH COLLEGE

Alleyn founded Dulwich College as a school for the poor and bequeathed the manor to it, and ever since that time the college has dominated the area and maintained its smart image. The original school building is now used as offices, and the buildings that now house the main school lie a little way to the south, designed in Renaissance style by Charles Barry, the son of the architect who was responsible for the Houses of Parliament. It is now a highly regarded independent day and boarding school for boys aged from seven to 18 and has close to 1,400 pupils. Old boys include Sir Ernest Shackleton, A E W Mason, P G Wodehouse, C S Forester, Raymond Chandler and Bob Monkhouse. Another distinction is that London's only surviving toll gate – now automatic – is maintained by Dulwich College.

*OPPOSITE The Victorian penchant for flamboyant ornamentation is preserved in the superb frontage of the 'new' Dulwich College buildings*

*RIGHT More serious and stolid by far, the original 17th-century buildings of Dulwich College no longer ring with the sounds of education in progress*

*The works of art on display at the Dulwich College Picture Gallery could have formed the nucleus of the National Gallery*

*BELOW The Horniman Museum is noted for its variety, and in particular for its collection of musical instruments from all over the world*

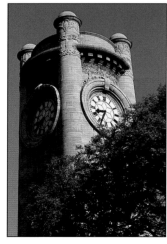

## DULWICH COLLEGE PICTURE GALLERY

The Dulwich College Picture Gallery, opened in 1817, is the oldest public art gallery in England, and contains a collection of some 300 Old Masters which form one of the best art collections in the world. These wonderful works of art are splendidly displayed in a purpose-built classical building, designed by Sir John Soane. They include Rembrandt's portrait of Jacob III de Gheyn (stolen several times from the gallery but, fortunately, recovered each time), Van Dyck's *Madonna and Child* and Poussin's *Return of the Holy Family from Egypt*. Some come from a substantial bequest by Sir Francis Bourgeois in 1811. His mausoleum is included in the building which, restored after wartime bomb damage, was redecorated to Soane's plans in the 1980s.

The works were originally intended to form the basis of a Polish National Gallery, and had been collected for the king of Poland by art dealer Noel Desenfans. The king was deposed before his gallery could be set up, whereupon Desenfans offered the paintings to the British Government, suggesting the founding of a new national gallery. Somewhat shortsightedly, they declined (though just a few years later, in 1824, they did indeed set up a National Gallery). Desenfans bequeathed the collection to his friend, Sir Francis Bourgeois, who in turn left it to the college.

## THE HORNIMAN MUSEUM AND PARK

Particularly popular with children, the Horniman Museum is a quirky collection which reflects the diverse interests of one man – the Quaker tea importer Frederick John Horniman, who travelled widely in the 1870s and collected anything that appealed to his sense of curiosity. Exhibits are wide ranging, from shrunken heads, tribal artefacts and Navaho sand

## CRYSTAL PALACE

◆

On a high hill just to the south of Dulwich, the Crystal Palace was re-erected in 1851, once it had served its purpose of housing the Great Exhibition in Hyde Park. The monumental glass and iron building, designed by Joseph Paxton, then became the centrepiece of a huge amusement park, opened by Queen Victoria in 1854. In 1936 the Crystal Palace went up in flames; 90 fire engines failed to quench the ferocity of the blaze. Today, all that remains of this vast Victorian Disneyland is the boating lake with some life-size models of prehistoric dinosaurs, made in 1854, set on a series of artificial islands. A small museum on Anerley Hill, near Crystal Palace station, covers the history of this fairy-tale building and its sad demise. The site does, however, continue to be used for various entertainments, since the park now houses a major athletics stadium and concert bowl where pop and orchestral concerts take place in summer.

*Three times the length of St Paul's Cathedral, Joseph Paxton's Crystal Palace was a magnificent symbol of Victorian achievement and success*

paintings to a stuffed walrus, natural history items and an important collection of musical instruments. Displays representing different cultures are skilfully arranged to illuminate a number of topics.

The museum is housed in an eccentric art nouveau building, and is surrounded by extensive grounds, with gardens, nature trails and enclosures with animals and birds. The park is especially colourful in May, when the azaleas and rhododendrons are in full bloom, but there are fine trees to admire at all times of the year, including statuesque oaks, some of which are at least 200 years old, and a number of more exotic specimens, such as the Japanese pagoda tree.

There is a path which leads south of the boating lake, café and aviary, and out by the lodge gates on Dulwich Common – once a royal hunting ground, but now catering for a new elite as an exclusive golf course.

## DULWICH VILLAGE

With the establishment of a spa at Dulwich Wells in the 18th century, there came an influx of big houses, then the Crystal Palace became a spur to fashionable development from the 1850s, and after that came the railways.

Handsome 18th-century houses, 19th-century villas and cottages cluster around the main streets, alongside attractive shops and restaurants. Charles Dickens used to come to meetings of the Dulwich Club (founded in 1772) at the old Greyhound pub, and he dispatched Mr Pickwick to live happily in Dulwich in his retirement.

# ·NORTH LONDON·

*I* f any area of London could be said to be quiet, perhaps it would be this one. The main streets are as full of traffic as anywhere, but it seems to be easier to escape them somehow, in the peaceful and elegant streets of Bloomsbury, the leafy avenues of St John's Wood or the quiet backwater of 'Little Venice'.

Many of the north London suburbs started life as rural villages, and some have managed to retain their own identity. Hampstead and Highgate are prime examples, where a village atmosphere combines with the smart status brought to these areas by a long list of distinguished residents, past and present. The homes of some of the more illustrious, including Sigmund Freud and Keats, are open as museums.

Other areas are becoming smart, as the demand for a decent London address increases. Places like Islington and Camden, which expanded rapidly and not too prettily during the age of steam railways and canal transport are being 'gentrified', but keep a lot of their colourful character with exceptionally good street markets and antiques shops

Closer to central London are the elegant terraces and crescents of the Regency redevelopment masterminded by John Nash and the Prince Regent, seen to its best advantage around Regents Park. The park was part of the plan, and is a delightful green space, incorporating the equally delightful London Zoo.

South of the park things get busier, with the great east–west route formed by Marylebone Road and Euston Road, and along here is one of Britain's most visited attractions – Madame Tussaud's and the adjacent Planetarium. Also along here are a clutch of great railway stations that carry passengers to all points north and west of the capital – King's Cross, St Pancras, Euston, Marylebone and Paddington. And yet, just a stone's throw away all is peace and quiet again in Bloomsbury, where the buildings of the University of London rub shoulders with the vast British Museum, a treasure-house of world history.

*George Gilbert Scott's 19th-century St Pancras station is a magnificent monument of neo-Gothic architecture, bristling with towers and spires*

# Regent's Park

 OST OF LONDON'S GREAT PARKS WERE GRADUALLY adapted over the centuries from former Royal hunting preserves or tracts of wild heathland, and Regent's Park is no exception. Tudor monarchs and their retinues would hunt here, and the area subsequently became a source of milk and hay for the capital. But Regent's Park is rather different from the others. It was created in the early 1800s as part of a huge and magnificent redevelopment scheme, the combined brainchild of the Prince Regent (hence the name) and architect John Nash, and was originally envisaged as a sumptuous private housing estate.

This part of the plan never came to fruition – only eight of the planned 56 villas were ever built – and though it is encircled by some of London's finest streets and splendid terraces, there remains in their midst this lovely green oasis.

*The gleaming, classical Cumberland Terrace, built in 1826-7 by John Nash and J Thomson, lies along the eastern side of Regent's Park*

The park is a lovely place for a stroll at any time of year, but is especially so in summer, when the roses and flower beds are at their best. The park also has a wealth of fine old trees and is exceptionally rich in bird life.

Sports facilities in the park include an athletics track, tennis courts and playing fields for cricket, rounders, hockey, softball, football and rugby, and to the west there is a large artificial boating lake, fed by the underground Tyburn stream, with rowing boats, canoes and kayaks for hire, together with a children's boating pond. Across Prince Albert Road is the Primrose Hill extension to Regent's Park, with a

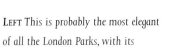

*ABOVE* The Inner Circle, now featuring
a delightful garden with lake and
cascade, was intended by Nash to be
the focus of the park development

151

*LEFT* This is probably the most elegant
of all the London Parks, with its
sweeping lawns, mature trees and
encircling classical terraces

summit that offers superb views across London, while around
Blomfield Road and Maida Avenue, on the other side of the
Regent's Canal, is 'Little Venice', with its waterside pubs,
villas and narrowboats.

## THE SOUTHERN PARK AND INNER CIRCLE

Nash's original plans are reflected in various parts of the
park. Those entering by the York Gate entrance can soon
stand on York Bridge and look back to see St Mary's Church,
on Marylebone High Street. When Nash laid out Regent's
Park he deliberately aligned the York Gate axis to take in a
view of the church, with its majestic Corinthian portico and
circular tower. York Bridge continues past Regent's College
on the left, now a centre for European studies and part of
Rochford College, Illinois, but formerly part of Bedford
College. It was founded in 1849 and was a pioneer of the
women's education movement. Beyond the college lies
Queen Mary's Garden, a circle filled with a colourful and
fragrant rose garden which was planted to honour Queen
Mary, the consort of George V. Here, too, is the Open Air
Theatre, which was founded in 1932 and is famous for its
productions of Shakespeare plays in summer.

*The finest Middle Eastern architecture, design and decoration have been used in the construction of the Central London Mosque*

152

## REGENT'S PARK MOSQUE

◆

In London's buildings expressions of ethnic diversity are as yet rare. Places of worship are one field in which new, consciously exotic buildings are springing up – notably mosques and temples. One of the best known is perhaps the Central London Mosque at Hanover Gate, Regent's Park, by Frederick Gibberd & Partners, its gilded dome and high minaret fitting in well with the sequence of Regency terraces, themselves rather exotic in places.

### THE OUTER CIRCLE

The Outer Circle road, close to the outer perimeter, is flanked at intervals by handsome Regency terraces, and close to the western edge is Winfield House, the United States Ambassador's residence, originally built for Barbara Hutton in 1937. Near by is the splendid London Central Mosque. Distinguished by its tall minaret and copper dome, the mosque was designed by Sir Frederick Gibberd and opened in 1978 as the principal Islamic mosque in Britain. It has a library, bookshop and offices, as well as a main hall designed to accommodate 1,800 worshippers.

Between the Outer Circle and the Regent's Canal, there are some fine new villas, designed by Quinlan Terry and completed in 1992. Named the Ionic, the Veneto and the Gothick, the buildings represent an example of the best of architectural craftsmanship.

### THE LONDON ZOOLOGICAL GARDENS

In the northern part of Regent's Park, with its main entrance on the Outer Circle, is London Zoo, which has delighted generations of families. In its heyday in the 1950s, more than 3 million visitors passed through its gates each year, but the zoo was never intended to exist purely to entertain. When it opened in 1828, the first institution of its kind in the world, it was dedicated to the study as well as the display of animals.

Unfortunately, financial considerations ultimately hold sway, and in the early 1990s, London Zoo found itself in the midst of such a financial crisis that the announcement was made that it would have to close. To the general population this was a great shock, and appeals for funds to save the zoo were quickly launched. Finally, with substantial help from the Emir of Kuwait, the zoo was saved, though its role has been redefined, with a far greater emphasis on conservation, education and the breeding of species that are endangered in

*The famous Penguin Pool at London Zoo provides an eminently suitable home for these delightful creatures, as well as excellent viewing facilities*

153

the wild, such as gorillas, Sumatran tigers and Asian lions. There are new displays designed to bring the task of conservation to life, explaining such projects as the Elephant Tracking Station, in which satellites are used to study the behaviour of wild herds and to give early warning of threats from ivory poachers. To emphasise man's impact on the natural world, there is a cage into which visitors are invited to step, and on it is the label, 'London Zoo presents the most destructive animal in the world'.

The original Zoological Society was founded in 1826 by Sir Stamford Raffles, who established the colony of Singapore, and Sir Humphry Davy. Within just a few years, they had opened a five-acre garden, and their own collection of exotic animals was soon joined by the royal menagerie from Windsor and the royal zoo from the Tower of London, forming the basis of what was to become one of the world's largest collections of animals.

The early layout and buildings, dating from 1827, were designed by Decimus Burton, and he began a tradition of imaginative zoo architecture that was later joined by the 1914 Mappin Terraces, the 1927 main gate and the famous 1930s Penguin Pool by Berthold Lubetkin. The Elephant and Rhino Pavilion, built in the mid-1960s is a superb example of Brutalist architecture, with textured concrete surfaces reflecting the bulky form and skin of its occupants. The walk-through Snowdon Aviary is of the same era, a huge and imaginative construction of steel and mesh which resembles nothing so much as a bird in flight and allows its occupants to fly freely. In the next decade, the Michael Sobell Pavilion for Apes and Monkeys was constructed, with tubular steel space-frame roofs acting as a substitute for a forest canopy.

In Moonlight World night and day have been reversed, so that nocturnal animals can be seen in an active state during the day, and the children's zoo is always a delight.

# *Marylebone*

*This entertaining sculpture of Shakespeare's Prospero and Ariel adorns the exterior of Broadcasting House, headquarters of the BBC*

*Opposite Park Crescent formed part of Nash's grand processional route between the Prince Regent's home, Carlton House and Regent's Park*

I N 1812 WORK BEGAN ON A BOLD SCHEME TO transform the West End of London and remodel the Crown-owned lands of Marylebone Park. John Nash, the Prince Regent's architect, cut a swathe through the heart of the metropolis, from Carlton House Terrace north via Regent Street and Portland Place, to Park Crescent. Beyond, he laid out the huge Regent's Park and intended to build a whole garden city of Italianate villas and grand terraces. The scheme was to make London a more beautiful city than Paris, and became, in part, a gesture of triumph following the defeat of Napoleon at Waterloo in 1815. The project was never completed in its entirety, but it left London with a new focus, a fine park and some of its best classical architecture. The rigid grid pattern of Marylebone's streets is broken by the serpentine shape of Marylebone Lane, which once threaded through the heart of the original medieval village of St Mary by the Bourne (the River Tyburn).

## Georgian Elegance

Marylebone is an area of contrasts, with Georgian elegance and a myriad shops and cafés. Along Portland Place, a wide and handsome street laid out by Robert Adam (1776–80) between Park Crescent and Regent Street, the best of the original houses, several serving as embassies, lie between Weymouth and New Cavendish Streets. Beyond are Broadcasting House, home of the BBC, and All Souls Church by John Nash, featuring the architectural mix of classical portico and Gothic spire. The rooftop restaurant at St George's Hotel offers extensive views over London. In Cavendish Square the best buildings are numbers 11–14 on the north side, built in 1770 and originally designed as part of a mansion for the Duke of Chandos. The archway between the two has a large bronze Madonna by Jacob Epstein. In Chandos Street, running north from the square, Chandos House (1771) is one of Adam's best designs. Harley Street, which also leads off Cavendish Square, has been synonymous with medicine since the mid-19th century. Medical practitioners, dentists, psychiatrists and cosmetic surgeons

## THE PLANETARIUM

◆

Beneath the green copper dome of the Planetarium, alongside Madame Tussaud's, the world of night and day are turned upside down. By day, the night sky is portrayed here as it is rarely seen in our real life world of street lights and atmospheric pollution. An extraordinarily complex Zeiss projector is used to beam a simulation of the stars and planets, which comes as quite a revelation to most visitors, and is accompanied by an excellent commentary. The adjacent Astronomer's Gallery uses audio-visual techniques to tell the story of scientists such as Galileo and Einstein, illustrating their contribution to our knowledge of the universe, and there are fascinating interactive displays which make the learning process great fun. After dark, the stars disappear, the Planetarium is transformed into the Laserium and the same dome gyrates to an exciting musical light and laser show.

*ABOVE RIGHT The entrance to Madame Tussaud's and the London Planetarium is a distinctive feature of Marylebone Road, as are the queues at times*

have their prestigious consulting rooms here, for the reception of wealthy private clients. Queen's College was founded here in 1848 as the first college of higher education for women in England.

## MADAME TUSSAUD'S

Madame Tussaud's is one of London's most popular tourist attractions, receiving well over a million visitors a year, and in the height of the summer season it can seem as if they are all in the queue! The Madame Tussaud's company has now opened similar waxworks displays in capital cities all over the world, but this is the original and the most fascinating of all, because of its range of historical exhibits. These include the genuine blade from the Paris guillotine – a grisly reminder of how this celebrated museum of wax figures began.

Madame Tussaud (1761–1850) perfected her craft during the French Revolution by taking death masks of guillotine victims, including Louis XVI and Marie Antoinette. In 1802 she fled Paris, and arrived in Britain with her macabre collection, first touring the country, then setting up an exhibition of historical figures, living and dead, in London in 1835. In 1884 the collection moved to Marylebone Road, where it has remained to this day. The oldest figure on display is Sleeping Beauty (1765), a portrait of Louis XV's mistress, Madame du Barry, which looks as if it is breathing. Madame Tussaud even modelled herself, and her self-portrait, created in 1842, can be seen in the Great Hall.

The collection is continually being extended to encompass famous figures from every age, but they are made using techniques that have changed little in 200 years.

## SHERLOCK HOLMES MUSEUM

◆

This small museum at 239 Baker Street (although the sign says 221B), lovingly created by the Sherlock Holmes International Society, is dedicated to Sir Arthur Conan Doyle's famous sleuth, one of the first fictional detectives. A recreation of the detective's home is furnished with his personal possessions and memorabilia from his most important cases. Fans of the Sherlock Holmes stories will remember that the address of his house was 221B Baker Street. The address was pure invention – no such house ever existed – but the site where it would have stood is marked by a plaque on the façade of the Abbey National bank. The Abbey National employs a full-time member of staff just to deal with the extraordinary number of letters that arrive from all over the world addressed to Holmes.

ABOVE *Sherlock Holmes would have approved of this creation of his study, if he or his famous address in Baker Street had ever existed at all*

LEFT *The chilling recreations within the Chamber of Horrors at Madame Tussaud's continue to hold a special fascination for visitors*

However, even in the waxworks time does not stand still – and neither do the models these days. Audio-animatronics have been introduced in the multi-million pound 'Spirit of London' experience, which recreates the sights, sounds and smells of the city as visitors glide by in 'time taxis'.

### THE CHAMBER OF HORRORS

The origins of the art of wax modelling have not been completely eclipsed by the swing towards the glittering showbusiness displays of movie stars and rock musicians. One of the most popular attractions at Madame Tussaud's is the Chamber of Horrors, which goes to great gruesome lengths to satisfy the human fascination with death and criminality. Exhibits include a working model of the guillotine, an electric chair and the gallows from Hertford Gaol, as well as the figures of notorious murderers. This taste for the distasteful is not new – The Duke of Wellington was a regular visitor to Madame Tussaud's and he particularly asked to be informed whenever any new exhibit was acquired by the Chamber of Horrors.

# The British Museum

THE BRITISH MUSEUM IS A TREASUREHOUSE OF THE arts and achievements of the world's civilisations, and it would take many visits to properly appreciate the full extent of its collections. One of the biggest attractions here is the Egyptian department, which contains one of the richest collections of ancient Egyptian art to be seen anywhere in the world. Other important sections include an impressive array of relics from ancient Greece, and nearly all of the most important archaeological treasures that have been unearthed in Britain can be seen within its walls. The subject matter is seemingly endless, and exhibits range from the priceless objects of ancient civilisations to amusing curiosities and the every-day artefacts of past times.

## AMASSING THE COLLECTIONS

The museum's origins go back to the 'curiosities' that were bequeathed to the nation in 1753 by the wealthy physician, Sir Hans Sloane, consisting largely of natural history specimens. The collection grew rapidly as a result of the Napoleonic Wars, following which the victorious British took

*The splendid frieze over the main entrance to the museum shows that the building was specially designed to hold the nation's treasures*

possession of many antiquities, including the Rosetta Stone, that the French had looted in Egypt. At the same time, the celebrated sculptures of the Parthenon and other important Greek works were 'collected' by the 7th Earl of Elgin and sold to the British government in 1816. A suitably monumental building was designed for their display in classical style by Sir Robert Smirke and completed in 1848. The museum is vast, covering an area of 13 acres (5.5 hectares), but some of the top attractions are conveniently close to the main entrance, including the contentious Elgin Marbles (Greece would like to have them back).

## TREASURES OF ANCIENT GREECE AND TURKEY

The most important of the Elgin Marbles is the so-called Parthenon Frieze, carved between 447 and 432 BC for the Temple of Athena, patroness of Athens. It originally ran around the interior wall of the temple colonnade, and it illustrates the procession that took place in the city every four years as part of a great festival in Athena's honour. Lord Elgin rescued about half of the original frieze – some 246ft (75m) in length – from the Parthenon ruins. Other parts had been shattered in 1687 when the Parthenon, used as an ammunitions store by occupying Turks, was hit by a shell and all but destroyed. Near by is the Room of the Caryatid,

The magnificent building which fronts
Great Russell Street was designed by
Sir Robert Smirke and constructed
between 1823 and 1852

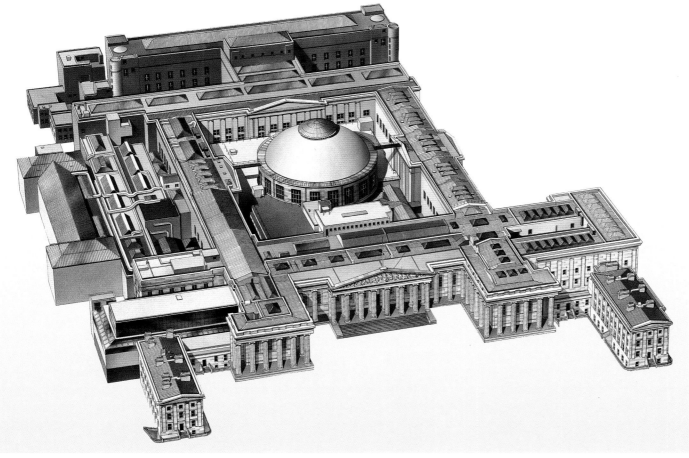

Smirke's original design for the
British Museum was soon adapted,
when the courtyard was converted into
the famous domed Reading Room

*The museum is particularly noted for its wonderful collection of architectural and other relics from the classical world*

## CURIOSITIES

◆

Of the more unusual items in the museum, one of the most popular exhibits is the perfectly preserved 2,000-year-old body of Lindow Man, nicknamed 'Pete Marsh' by the archaeologists who found him in a waterlogged peat bog in Cheshire. The fascination with corpses continues with the ancient Egyptian coffins and their contents – not just human mummies, but also those of sacred animals, including crocodiles, cats, dogs, fish, an ape, an ibex and even a bull. Less gruesome are the early games, including dice, mosaic gaming board and counters from ancient Babylon, which were made around 2600 BC, and the mid-12th century Lewis chessmen, beautifully carved in ivory. Clocks, watches and musical timepieces form another interesting display – many are still working, and all chime together on the hour.

named after the figure of a maiden of the 5th century BC, one of a series of columns from the Erectheion in Athens (a shrine to the mythical king Erectheus). Room 12 contains what little survives of one of the Seven Wonders of the Ancient World – the Mausoleum of Halicarnassus. Brought from Turkey, it consists of sculptural fragments from the great tomb built for Mausolus, Prince of Caria, by his wife in the 4th century BC. Mausolus himself is depicted, and a figure that could possibly be his wife, as well as a battle between the Greeks and Amazons.

### THE EGYPTIAN COLLECTION

Some of the best objects in the museum are displayed in Room 25. At the southern end is the celebrated Rosetta Stone, named after the town near the mouth of the Nile where it was found in 1799. The insignificant-looking slab unlocked the secret of ancient Egyptian hieroglyphs – its

TOP *The Elgin Marbles are starkly displayed, but adequately speak for themselves; above, one of the marbles portrays the Horse of Selene*

*The museum's Reading Room is as full of atmosphere as it is of books, and many famous scholars and writers have frequented it over the years*

inscription has a Greek translation alongside, allowing scholars to work from the known back to the unknown. Among all the other very fine tombs and statues is a naturalistic cat in bronze (wearing nose and ear rings) displayed in one of the central cases.

### EUROPEAN HISTORY

On the upper floor of the museum, a series of rooms tells the story of Europe and the British Isles from early prehistory to the end of the Middle Ages. There are displays that throw light on London's early history, including the superb

Battersea Shield – a fine example of Celtic Art of the mid-1st century BC – and the tombstone of Julius Classicianus, the Roman official who governed London from AD 61 to 65. Near by is the Mildenhall Treasure, a complete set of silver embossed tableware dating from the 4th century, so magnificent that it must have belonged to a Roman governor or another high official. Best of all is the Sutton Hoo Treasure, consisting of bejewelled swords, helmets, buckles, bowls, drinking horns and a bronze cauldron. They were all excavated from a 7th-century ship burial, most probably that of Redwald, King of the East Angles, and they provide convincing

2095

## THE READING ROOM

◆

The British Museum was originally built around an open courtyard. Not long after the building was finished, it was decided to make better use of this space by roofing it over to create the famous round Reading Room. Since it opened in 1857 many precious books have been consulted here — by Carlyle and Lenin amongst others — and several important books written, including *Das Kapital*, the political and economic manifesto of Karl Marx (his usual seat in the Reading Room was number G7). A new set of books is due to fill its shelves, for the museum's library is to move to a new building, and the space may then be used for the Museum of Mankind's books on travel, anthropology and ethnology.

over India and south-east Asia, some gently erotic, some serenely mystic. Below, in Room 34, is the collection of Islamic art, including a variety of miniatures depicting garden scenes, hunting and courting couples in exquisite colour. There are also displays on scientific ideas which the West absorbed from the Islamic world via Moorish Spain.

### ASSYRIAN ART

The rooms in the British Museum devoted to Assyrian art are less well known than the Greek antiquities but are no less striking. They include a huge winged lion that once guarded the palace and temple complex at Nimrud, built around 880 BC, and the theme of the lion-hunt features in several narrative friezes, notably the sculptures from the throne room at Nimrud, and some magnificent carvings from the palace at Nineveh (7th-century BC). These latter scenes seem almost modern in their clean, fluid lines and the naturalistic portrayal of wounded lions writhing in agony.

evidence that the raiders who settled in England during the so-called Dark Ages were not the uncouth barbarians of popular imagination, but were highly skilled craftsmen.

### THE ORIENTAL ART COLLECTION

Some of the British Museum's best galleries are among the quietest and least visited, because they lie furthest from the main entrance. The back door, round the corner on Montague Place, leads straight to Room 33, part of which is devoted to a chronological account of Chinese art. The rest of the room contains a striking collection of sculpture from temples all

*This covered silver bowl forms part of the exquisite 4th-century Mildenhall Treasure, and still shows the quality and artistry of the craftsmanship*

# Bloomsbury and Fitzrovia

BLOOMSBURY, LYING TO THE EAST OF TOTTENHAM COURT Road, is a district of leafy squares, dominated by buildings that house the faculties of the University of London, and also by the British Museum. The area is associated with a circle of writers who set the pace for artistic and intellectual life in the early decades of this century, and who became known collectively as the Bloomsbury Group, because some of their members (including Virginia Woolf, Vanessa Bell, Lytton Strachey and John Maynard Keynes) had homes in the district. Fitzrovia, to the west, was the haunt of hard-drinking Bohemian writers, journalists and artists in the 1940s and '50s (including Dylan Thomas, George Orwell, Cyril Connolly and Anthony Burgess); these writers were the first to coin the name Fitzrovia to suggest the antithesis of genteel Belgravia.

## DICKENS' HOUSE

Charles Dickens, the great 19th-century novelist, is one of that handful of writers who have shaped and moulded our vision of London. His descriptions of the fog-bound haunts of torpid lawyers, of the criminal underworld of Fagin and his thieves or the cramped and crooked home of Little Nell, the Old Curiosity Shop, are as vivid now as they were 150 years ago. It only takes a little imagination to conjure up visions of Dickensian London as you wander the city's streets, and a visit to Dickens' house allows you to pursue the illusion.

*Bloomsbury Square, more the size of a park, was the first of all the London squares, its gardens laid out by Humphrey Repton in about 1800*

The house is the only surviving London home out of several in which the author lived and worked. He moved here in 1837, a year after his marriage to Catherine Hogarth, but by 1839, such was Dickens' growing wealth that the family was able to move on to 1 Devonshire Terrace (since demolished), a more impressive house overlooking Regent's Park. In the time that Dickens lived here he was characteristically prolific: he completed *The Pickwick Papers*, wrote *Oliver Twist* and *Nicholas Nickleby* and began *Barnaby Rudge* all in under three years.

His house, which was bought by the Dickens Fellowship in 1924, retains the heavy Victorian colour scheme and the desk and chair where Dickens wrote, surrounded by the hustle and bustle of family life – he possessed the remarkable talent of being able to write even with the distractions of noise, visitors and conversation all around him. Other Dickens memorabilia on display includes first editions of his work, the copies he used for his public readings, still marked with his prompt points, and Lionel Bart's score for his musical version of *Oliver Twist*.

ABOVE *Bedford Square is typical of this part of London, lined with impressive terraces and displaying a quiet and distinguished charm*

## THOMAS CORAM FOUNDATION

The Thomas Coram Foundation (once known as the Foundling Hospital) was set up to provide shelter and an education for orphaned and abandoned children. Its founder was the remarkable Captain Thomas Coram, shipbuilder and master mariner, who played an important role in the colonisation of Massachusetts, Georgia and Nova Scotia. Returning to London in 1732, he was appalled by the sight of abandoned children and infants 'left to die on dung-hills'. He devoted the remainder of his life to working on their behalf, establishing the Foundling Hospital, with George II and many other eminent figures of the age as patrons. The present building, on the same site, dates from 1937. Its walls are hung with paintings given by well-wishers, most notably those of William Hogarth (who was one of the first governors). Many of the works are on charitable themes or depict Biblical subjects related to the hospital's work. The highlight of the collection, however, is Hogarth's masterful portrait of the founder, Captain Thomas Coram (1740). The Courtroom, where the present governors still hold their meetings, is a reproduction of the original, with an ornate plaster ceiling and cases containing good-luck tokens and charms left by impoverished mothers with the illegitimate babies they abandoned on London's streets. Handel was another strong supporter of the hospital's work in the courtroom and you can see the score of the *Messiah* which he donated, and the keyboard of the organ on which he gave fund-raising recitals.

LEFT *Russell Square, near the back of the British Museum, is the largest of Bloomsbury's squares and is at the very heart of the university area*

# Camden and Islington

*N*ORTH OF EUSTON AND ST PANCRAS STATIONS, CUT BY railway lines and the Regent's Canal, Camden Town offers 'a lovely bunch' of markets. Entirely rural until the end of the 18th century, its development really began in the 1820s and 1830s with the coming of the canal and railways. There was substantial Irish immigration from the later-19th century, and the Greek Cypriot influx which began in the 1920s gathered strength from the 1950s; from the 1970s there has been a steady movement towards 'gentrification'. The area was in St Pancras borough until 1965, when the Borough of Camden was formed by joining the older boroughs of Holborn, St Pancras and Hampstead.

At the Camden Lock Centre former canal buildings have been converted into shops, craft workshops and cafés to form a pleasant and interesting shopping centre which was opened in 1973. The centre features a weekend market and boat trips are available on Regent's Canal.

*Rummaging around the stalls of antiques and bric-a-brac at Camden Lock Market is a favourite weekend pastime for Londoners and visitors*

## MERRY ISLINGTON

North of the City on the Great North Road, 'merry Islington' was a village on a hill providing an enjoyable day out from London and supplying the capital with dairy products and water. Suburban development began late in the 18th century. The 19th century brought the Regent's Canal, the railways, commuters and slums. The area has attracted much Irish immigration in Victorian times and since, and enjoyed a process of gentrification from the 1960s. Indeed, within its mix of smart and run-down areas, Islington contains some splendid houses and lovely little squares and has a lively entertainment scene. The older Boroughs of Islington and Finsbury were combined in 1965.

167

## REGENT'S CANAL
◆

The Regent's Canal is a branch of the Grand Union Canal, cut between 1812 and 1820 through the north of London from the Paddington Basin to Limehouse, where it met the Thames. It was once the busiest of Britain's inland waterways, carrying goods from all over the country on the last leg of the journey to London docks. Today it is a quiet backwater, dedicated to leisure pursuits, and narrowboat cruises with commentaries are run by the London Waterbus Company. The Regent's Canal Information Centre in Camden High Street is in an old lock-keeper's cottage. It describes the canal's history and maps out its route and sells excellent guides to its walks and wildlife.

*Camden Market represents a fine example of how formerly run-down canal areas have been revitalised and developed for shopping and leisure*

## THE ANGEL

The Angel, Islington is a famous former coaching inn on the Great North Road, located at the centre of the area's shopping district, on the corner of Islington High Street and Pentonville Road. There has been an inn on the site from 1638. The hostelry was a popular overnight stay for travellers arriving late from North who preferred not to risk the highwaymen and footpads on the dark road into the City itself. Tom Paine was said to have written *The Rights of Man* there and the inn is mentioned in *Oliver Twist* as the place where visitors from the north felt that London really began. Rebuilt in 1880, it was a Lyons Corner House from 1921 to 1959, and subsequently a bank.

*Canonbury Square is a delightful haven amidst the busy streets of Islington, with colourful formal borders and ornamental trees*

# Hampstead

H IGH UP ON ITS HILL, THE MEDIEVAL VILLAGE OF Hampstead stood among woods, but these had largely been cleared by the end of the 17th century. Later, it became a fashionable spa and the settlement grew, but Hampstead managed to retain its pretty lanes and village atmosphere. This, together with its vast expanse of semi-rural heath, has attracted many eminent writers, politicians and intellectuals over the years. Anna Pavlova, the ballerina, Sigmund Freud, the father of pyschoanalysis and the Romantic poet, John Keats, are among past residents whose homes have now been made into museums.

The tone of the area is intellectual, up-market and liberal. Several well-known left-wing writers and politicians live here – 'champagne socialists', who live pampered lives while espousing egalitarianism. Bishop's Avenue, the local Millionaire's Row, features grandiose and gigantically expensive modern houses.

### AROUND HAMPSTEAD STREETS

Hampstead High Street has good bookshops, boutiques and restaurants – and the deepest underground station in London, which lies 192ft (58.5m) below street level. It served as an air-raid shelter during World War II.

Clustered around the High Street is an intricate maze of attractive lanes. Heath Street descends southwards to Church Row, with its Georgian houses fronted by iron railings, and halfway down the Row is the parish church of St John (1744–7), topped by a bold spire. Inside are memorials to many former Hampstead residents, including Keats, the architect Norman Shaw, John Constable, the artist, and the novelist George du Maurier.

Fenton House, in Hampstead Grove, is a 17th-century residence which is open to the public. Built in William and Mary style in 1695, it contains beautiful period furnishings, English and European porcelain and a collection of 17th- and 18th-century keyboard instruments, including a harpsichord of 1612, which may have belonged to Handel. A network of little lanes run around Hampstead Grove, and many of the

*Flask Walk is a charming street of Georgian houses where once there were the baths and pump room of the Hampstead spa*

## HAMPSTEAD SPA

◆

Hampstead became a fashionable spa in the 18th century, and the Vale of Health, an area and street in the south-west of East Heath, was named to attract residents. These included the writer Leigh Hunt and, more recently, historians J C and Barbara Hammond, D H Lawrence and Rabindranath Tagore. Well Walk was the heart of the spa, with its pump room and assembly rooms standing on the site of the mineral spring. John Constable lived at Number 40, socialist H M Hyndman at Number 13, Marie Stopes at Number 14, J B Priestley at Number 27, D H Lawrence at Number 32 and architect Ewan Christian at Number 50.

houses display blue plaques recording the names of their eminent former residents.

In New End is Burgh House, which was built in 1703 by the physician Dr Gibbons. Its rooms are now used for art exhibitions and local history displays, as well as being a venue for talks, exhibitions and concerts by local musicians, and there is a good café in the basement.

Near by, Flask Walk and Well Walk are reminders that Londoners once came here to take the waters at the Pump House, which has since disappeared. In Flask Walk, the Flask Tavern was the meeting place of the Kit-Cat Club in the early 18th century, a political and literary group whose members included Britain's first prime minister, Robert Walpole, the essayists, Addison and Steele, and Sir John Vanbrugh, the celebrated playwright and architect.

*Church Row, a superb example of Georgian architecture, is frequently hailed as Hampstead's finest street, and St John's Church is worth a visit*

*Hampstead Heath, once the haunt of Highwaymen, is now a prized and fiercely protected tract of amenity land, with splendid views over London*

### A Poet's Abode

Keats' Grove (formerly known as Wentworth Grove) is the location of the Keats' House Museum. John Keats came to live here in 1818, fell in love with his next door neighbour, Fanny Brawne, and became engaged to her in 1819. In 1820 he left for Italy for the good of his health, and died there in 1821. During the short time he lived in this house he wrote some of his best-loved poems, including Ode to a Nightingale; the plum tree under which he wrote this poem has gone, but a recent replacement in the garden marks the spot. The rest of the house displays books, letters, manuscripts and personal items which belonged to Keats and Fanny Brawne, and the furnishings are all in period style.

### Hampstead Heath

In 1829, Hampstead's Lord of the Manor, Sir Thomas Wilson, wanting to capitalise on the popularity of the village, produced a scheme to build new houses all over the vast heath that he owned to the north of the village. This caused uproar, and opposition to the scheme raged for 40 years until, at Wilson's death in 1869 conservationists finally won the battle to save the Heath for public enjoyment. It is a vast nature reserve, home to more than 80 species of birds as well as foxes, rabbits and rare wild service trees, and extends across Spaniards Road to the Sandy Heath woods, the Hampstead Heath Extension (added in 1907), West Heath and Golders

Hill Park. The Heath is also a public playground where Londoners come to walk, jog, ride their horses and enjoy picnics. Nearby Parliament Hill offers extensive views over central London – local legend claims that Queen Boudicca (Boadicea), the Iron-Age ruler who fought against the Roman conquest of Britain, lies buried beneath the hill. Another story claims that Guy Fawkes' fellow conspirators planned to watch the explosion of Parliament from here. This is also a favourite kite-flying spot, and there is a lido with a huge swimming pool. Also for swimmers are the three ponds to the east of the Heath – Kenwood Pond for women, Highgate Pond for men and Hampstead Pond for mixed bathing.

### DELIGHTS OF THE EAST

◆

Moving west from Hampstead Heath, in the unfashionable area of Neasden, a magnificent Hindu temple, Shri Swaminarayan Mandir, was completed in 1995. Its assembly hall, with a capacity of 2,500 people, is the largest in Europe. It was developed by and for the local Hindu community and is faithful to a thousand-year tradition of design in timber and stone. In addition to those few already existing, London will certainly see more such architectural expressions of ethnic diversity; the challenge will be to combine these traditions agreeably with traditional London townscape.

*OPPOSITE The Shri Swaminarayan Mandir temple has brought the magnificence of Hindu architecture to the otherwise far from exotic area of Neasden*

# Highgate

*The western section of Highgate Cemetery is the oldest, and contains some fine monuments and statuary amidst lush vegetation*

*The most famous grave in the whole of Highgate Cemetery is undoubtedly that of Karl Marx, united (at least in death) with the workers of the world*

SINCE THE EARLY 19TH CENTURY THE SUBURBS OF London have crept northwards, swallowing up lesser settlements, but Highgate has clung on to its village atmosphere and its up-market tone. The hub of Highgate village is around Pond Square, which has a delightful mixture of Georgian cottages, grander houses, small shops and restaurants. To one side is the Flask pub, so called because travellers would stop here to fill their flasks with drink for the journey ahead. At first, Highgate Hill is something of a contrast, with its bleak, ugly hospital buildings, but these soon give way to houses with elegant Georgian façades. Opposite these, a long wall separates the road from the peaceful oasis of Waterlow Park, a hillside garden with fine views to Regent's Park and central London. Towards the top of the park, Lauderdale House, built in 1645 and briefly the home of Nell Gwyn, Charles II's mistress, is open to the public. There are more Georgian houses in The Grove, a little to the north, where the poet Samuel Taylor Coleridge lived.

## HIGHGATE CEMETERY

Highgate Cemetery opened in 1839 as a commercial enterprise, run by the London Cemetery Company, selling burial plots with a guarantee that the occupants of the graves would remain undisturbed (it was common practice in those days for remains to be dug up to make way for new burials). It proved to be immensely popular, and a much-needed alternative to overcrowded churchyards, where tomb-robbing was a problem. However, in time, with all the burial plots sold and no revenue for maintenance, the cemetery became sadly neglected, and nature took control of the site. Happily, the Friends of Highgate Cemetery came to the rescue in the 1970s, and thanks to their efforts the site today has the added attraction of being an important nature reserve.

It is unusual, to say the least, for a suburban cemetery to be a popular tourist attraction, but Highgate has that distinction, partly for its splendid Victorian landscaping and funerary architecture, but mostly because of the number of famous names that can be found on the headstones.

Straddling Swain's Lane, the cemetery has been a visitor attraction ever since it opened. The earliest part is the western section, which has an imposing entrance, the Egyptian Avenue, Circle of Lebanon and catacombs, and the colossal 1880s mausoleum of Julius Beer by John Oldrid Scott. This part, only open for guided tours, contains the graves of such luminaries as Michael Faraday, Sir John Betjemen, Charles Dickens' wife and Elizabeth Siddal, the beautiful wife of Dante Gabriel Rossetti. Rossetti buried a volume of unpublished poems with his wife, but later had a change of heart, seeking permission to open the grave so that his work could be recovered and published.

## TURN AGAIN

◆

Now the stuff of pantomime and children's story books, the tale of Dick Whittington does have a flimsy grasp on historical fact. According to the legend, Dick rested with his cat on his way out of London, having failed to make his fortune in the city. Three times, as he rested, he thought he heard the Bow Bells chime 'Turn again, Whittington, thrice Mayor of London', and on the third occasion he decided to return. In reality, Richard Whittington was born the son of a Gloucestershire squire. He was, indeed, three times Mayor of London (in 1397, 1406 and 1419) but the fable of his rags-to-riches rise seems to have been invented in the 17th century, 200 years after Whittington's death. Whether or not he ever paused on Highgate Hill is therefore a matter for debate, but the Whittington Stone, set by the roadside, is there for all to see.

The eastern section, which was added in the 1850s, is open to visitors, and with more than 50,000 graves, it is the last resting place of many distinguished Londoners. The best known grave here is that of Karl Marx, who died in Hampstead in 1883. His last resting place is marked by a monumental bust of Marx (by Laurence Bradshaw, 1956) and the inscription, 'Workers of all lands unite'.

## KENWOOD HOUSE

Just a few minutes walk from the centre of Highgate is the splendid stately home, Kenwood House, gloriously situated in wooded grounds to the north of Hampstead Heath. It was built in the early 17th century, but was remodelled 150 years later by Robert Adam, and was bequeathed to the nation in 1927 by the 1st Earl of Iveagh, head of the Guinness family.

The Iveagh Bequest included the outstanding collection of paintings which are still displayed here. Rembrandt's brooding *Portrait of the Artist* (c1665), Vermeer's *The Guitar Player* (c1676) and Gainsborough's fine portrait of Lady Howe (c1764) are among many other important works by English and Dutch masters.

Open-air concerts are given in the grounds, by the lake, on Saturday evenings in June, July and August, with fireworks after some performances.

*The perfect proportions of Kenwood House provide a splendid backdrop for the popular open-air concerts held in the grounds in the summer*

# Index

175

# Acknowledgements

The Automobile Association would like to thank the following photographers, libraries and museums for their assistance in the preparation of this book:

ARCAID 16/7 (Richard Bryant), 17a & 17b (Lucinda Lambton), 40/1 (Richard Bryant), 40 (Mark Fiennes), 87 (J Cockayne), 97 (Richard Bryant), 140/1 (Martin Jones), 145 (Dennis Gilbert), 168/9, 169 & 171 (David Churchill)
THE BRIDGEMAN ART LIBRARY 2/3 The Great Fire of London, 1666 by Dutch School, 17th century (Museum of London), 20b Hampton Court, engraving from Havell's 'History of the Thames', 1793 by Joseph Farington, 1747–1821 (Guildhall Library, Corporation of London), 22/3 Hampton Court Palace: Rebuilt by Christopher Wren during the reign of William and Mary, 1690–1702 (John Bethell), 24 The King's Staircase, 17th century (Hampton Court Palace, Surrey), 33 Richmond Bridge by Myles Birket Foster, 1825–99 (Guildhall Art Gallery, Corporation of London), 38 Kensington Palace: The King's Staircase, 56/7 Buckingham Palace, London, completed in 1828 by John Nash (1752–1835), Admiralty Arch, executed 1911 (John Bethell)
© THE BRITISH MUSEUM, LONDON 162
BRITSTOCK-IFA LTD 64/5 reverse
C M DIXON 161b
THE DORCHESTER 95
EDIFICE 86/7, 98/9, 101a & 117 (Darley), 146/7, 150 (Lewis)
MARY EVANS PICTURE LIBRARY 147
ROBERT HARDING PICTURE LIBRARY LTD 55a, 94a, 106/7
THE IMAGE BANK 74a, 76a, 78b, 122, 124/5, 136b
IMAGES COLOUR LIBRARY LTD 134, 134/5, 172/3
RICHARD KALINA 138a
MUSEUM OF THE MOVING IMAGE 137a
PHOTOGRAPHERS INTERNATIONAL PICTURE LIBRARY 61b
PICTURES COLOUR LIBRARY LTD 6, 12, 12/3, 14a, 14b, 14/5, 32/3, 39a, 42a, 66/7, 68a, 71, 74b, 74/5, 78a, 79, 118b, 120b, 150/1, 158/9, 166, 166/7, 167

REX FEATURES LTD 50, 64 facing, 64, 64/5, 65a, 121a, 161a, 162/3
THE ROYAL COLLECTION © HER MAJESTY THE QUEEN 58, 59, 60
SCIENCE MUSEUM, LONDON 44, 45
SPECTRUM COLOUR LIBRARY 16, 19a, 19b, 30, 69, 70, 73, 80/1a, 113, 114a
J SPELLER 34a
TONY STONE IMAGES F/Cover, 8/9 reverse, 104/5 reverse
TATE GALLERY, LONDON 62/3 (Marcus Leith), 63a
MADAME TUSSAUDS 157b
© TRUSTEES OF THE VICTORIA & ALBERT MUSEUM 116a, 116b
ZEFA PICTURES 21, 51, 52/3, 65 facing, 76b, 94b, 118a, 120/1 reverse, 120a facing

All remaining pictures are held in the Association's own library (AA PHOTO LIBRARY) with contributions from the following photographers:

P BAKER 119a; T COHEN 72/3; R DAY 44/5, 93; P ENTICKNAP 110/1; D FORSS 8a facing, 20a, 25; P KENWARD 8e, 8f, 18, 36, 39b, 46, 48, 82, 88a, 88b, 89, 92, 100, 106, 108a, 112, 126, 127b, 128, 128/9, 129, 136a, 137b, 138b, 138c, 139a, 139b, 152a, 152b, 156/7, 165; |S & O MATHEWS 84, 98b, 164/5, 170; R MORT 9i, 26a, 28/9, 34/5, 108b, 119b, 144, 151, 164; B SMITH B/Cover, 26b, 26/7, 29a, 29b, 42/3, 104 facing, 142; R STRANGE 30/1, 36/7, 42b, 47a, 47b, 54a, 55b, 90, 92/3, 99, 122/3, 154/5, 154, 157a, 158; J A TIMS 96; M TRELAWNY 9, 9g, 35a, 35b, 98a, 101b, 101c, 111, 121a facing, 143a, 148, 152/3, 160, 172a; R VICTOR 72, 102, 127a; W VOYSEY 9a facing, 9d facing, 67, 80, 120a, 121b facing, 132, 143b; P WILSON 83, 90/1; P WOODCOCK 105 facing, 109, 114b, 130b, 131b, 146; A WOOLFITT 54/5, 80/1b; G WRONA 8d, 114/5

Illustrations by MALTINGS PARTNERSHIP (held in AA PHOTO LIBRARY).